PUTTING
FORGIVENESS
INTO PRACTICE

DORIS DONNELLY

Argus Communications
A Division of DLM, Inc.
Allen, Texas 75002 U.S.A.

All biblical quotations are from *The Jerusalem Bible*, copyright © 1966 by Darton, Longman & Todd, Ltd. and Doubleday & Company, Inc. Used by permission of the publisher.

Summary and quotation from Karl Menninger, M.D., *Whatever Became of Sin?* (New York: Hawthorn Books, 1973), pp. 134-71. Reprinted by permission of E. P. Dutton, Inc.

Designed and illustrated by Jerry Kenney

Argus Communications
A Division of DLM, Inc.
One DLM Park
Allen, Texas 75002 U.S.A.

Printed in the United States of America

International Standard Book Number: 0-89505-087-0

Library of Congress Catalog Card Number: 82-71967

0 9 8 7 6 5 4 3 2 1

*For
Chris &
Peggy*

Contents

Introduction

This book exists because of a conviction that is so real to me that it had to take form and a life of its own in the shape of these pages. The conviction is that forgiveness is an underused but powerful force in our personal lives as well as in the families, communities, and even nations that claim us as part of them.

Forgiveness makes the difference between war and peace, hatred and love, hope and despair. Without forgiveness, hurts grow unchecked and we recycle failures, resentments, bitterness, and mistrust in our lives. With forgiveness, hurts are acknowledged and healed, and we are able to break a mindless cycle of retaliation by saying that the decisions of human life, even when they turn out badly, are not beyond repair. Martin Luther King, Jr., put it this way: "Forgiveness is a catalyst creating the atmosphere necessary for a fresh start and a new beginning." I believe— *I know*—that is so.

The conviction that prompted me to write this book is not merely theoretical. I have come to see that the subject of forgiveness touches everyone's life. Sometimes that contact is direct and immediate: there is someone from whom forgiveness is needed or who needs to be forgiven. Sometimes we are physically or emotionally near someone who is struggling with forgiveness and who asks our support in the process. Sometimes an association or a relationship from the past haunts our present behavior and decisions, and we need to renew our forgiving spirit so that a more complete healing occurs. There are times when we need to forgive ourselves or God; still other times we need to experience the assurance of God's pardon. In some instances, we may see that forgiveness needs to be mediated on a large scale between families, communities, and even between nations so that a real, not pretended, peace can take hold.

You may notice a consistent connection between forgiveness and peacemaking in the following pages. This is so because I believe that forgiveness is the essential ingredient that allows peace to be. Sometimes in our eagerness to patch up differences, we rush toward reconciliations without taking account of what has to be forgiven. When that happens, the truces made and peace treaties signed are often broken before the ink is dry. There has to be a pause between the hurt and reconciliation so that forgiveness can take place. Without forgiveness, there can be no real peace and no lasting reconciliation.

I do not know what particular set of circumstances led you to this book. Regardless of the route, I believe you will find in the following chapters and exercises a means to live more freely and peacefully by putting forgiveness into practice.

Because of the range of situations that forgiveness touches, it will be up to you to make yourself at home with this book—reading what most appeals and pertains to you and "exercising" where your interests lead. There is special value, I think, in sharing your discoveries with someone else, and I encourage you to do this if at all possible.

Your comments, suggestions, questions, and reflections, addressed to me in care of the publisher, will reach me and allow me to respond personally to you. I welcome hearing from you.

Doris Donnelly
December 8, 1981

CHAPTER 1

Where Do We *Begin?*

Identifying Our Hurts

Charity begins at home because hurt begins at home. Forgiveness begins at home, too, because forgiveness is a special kind of love that asks us to remain open, vulnerable, and caring even though we have been wounded, offended, hurt, or pained.

People serious about the process of forgiveness will be helped by scanning whatever is or has been "home base" for most of each day over the years. Usually, that will mean recalling family relationships as children growing up; peer, neighbor, family, and school relationships through childhood and adolescence; significant personal, social, and career relationships later on. Through all of this, the idea is to recall people (singly or in groups), institutions, societies, governments, corporations, communities as well as situations that have been occasions of hurt *to* us or hurt *by* us.

For some, the process of healing begins at whatever is home base now: a family conflict, hurt at school, tension at work, misunderstandings with neighbors or friends. For others, the process of forgiving will involve reaching back in memories and dealing with an event or person of the past. Some of those persons and events will be obvious, some will trigger memories so negative that it will be instinctive to resist their scrutiny, and some hurts will be subtle and camouflaged but unyielding in their destructive effects unless checked and healed.

Whatever these hurts are and wherever they are found, it is important to identify them, not to reopen old wounds but to free us from their weighty hold on us so that peace can root itself in our hearts.

Testing Our Hurts

Once you are able to identify your hurts, it is helpful and even necessary to "test" them. It is important to know that the hurts you have identified as in need of healing and forgiveness are your real hurts and that forgiveness is directed properly.

Once there was a businessman who believed he had to forgive his secretary for delinquent and sloppy reports submitted in his name until he "tested" his forgiveness story with an associate and came to see that he really had to forgive *himself* for not having the reports ready in time to be typed precisely and written well enough to merit the praise he yearned for.

It is not difficult to blame a teacher for something that is really our responsibility *or* to take responsibility for something that a teacher was obliged to do! Determining who and what have to be forgiven is a very enlightening follow-up to your survey of hurts at home base. To neglect that verification is to run the risk of spending energy and effort forgiving or asking forgiveness for the wrong thing.

Testing is often best done by reviewing your situation with someone who knows you and who cares about you. You need someone who is a good listener—honest and patient. It goes without saying that someone who is anxious to move the core of hurt and forgiveness away from you ("It wasn't your fault," "It could have happened to anyone," etc.) in order to spare you pain isn't the most helpful confidant in this confirmation exercise.

People who pray and those who have achieved a degree of self-knowledge and self-acceptance are often able to determine by some inner verifier of these things when they have acknowledged the "right" hurt or when they are avoiding or delaying the inevitable. One way or another, the testing process must be done.

If several places in need of forgiveness emerge in scanning home base and its confirmation process, dealing with one situation at a time is a generally recommended procedure.

Some Ground Rules   Like other procedures in life, forgiving has a few preliminary ground rules. These ground rules are especially important to consider in the beginning stages of forgiveness because forgiveness is neither natural, instinctive, nor logical, and it is usually very difficult. In fact, forgiveness frequently appears to be such a bizarre, ludicrous, weak, and even scandalous activity that it is often abandoned as an *idea* before it ever becomes a *practice*.

These ground rules, then, are meant to encourage a difficult process and to pave the way for getting forgiveness off the ground and on its way:

1. It isn't necessary to tell the person you are forgiving that he or she is the subject of your efforts. If sharing that information will help, do it. If sharing that information will exacerbate an already difficult situation, avoid it. The same rule of thumb holds true *after* forgiveness occurs. You have no obligation to tell the person you have forgiven that you have done so. It is helpful to do so in some situations and not helpful in others.

2. Forgiveness is just as hard to receive as to give. In both cases, forgiving involves an "owning" of the person and a "disowning" of the offense. "Forgiving," wrote the Jewish philosopher Hannah Arendt in *The Human Condition*, ". . . is always an eminently personal (though not necessarily individual or private) affair in which *what* was done is forgiven for the sake of *who* did it."

   The most strenuous effort is involved in doing that kind of separating when the offense looms so large that it defines the other (or you, when you are the one in need of forgiveness).

   ✳ Forgiveness is difficult *to give* because you need to see the one who hurt you as other than the hurt, and that isn't easy.

   ✳ Forgiveness is difficult *to receive* because you need to believe that someone has seen more in you than whatever hurtful thing it is that you did. Furthermore, *you* need to believe the same about yourself—which is another way of saying that you are deserving of forgiveness.

3. Even though the person who hurt you and is in need of your forgiveness (or vice versa) is distanced geographically or has died, it is never too late or impossible to forgive.

3

It took twenty-five years before Michelangelo could forgive a rival for deliberately defacing a set of his drawings. The cruelty associated with that act of vandalism led Michelangelo into a lengthy depression and period of moroseness. When he was finally able to forgive, the man who had committed the act was already dead, but that did not lessen the possibility or the importance of the reconciliation for Michelangelo.

The point is that forgiveness applies to the living and the dead, the proximate and the distanced. It has no geographic or time barriers.

4. Suppose a salesclerk slights you, or an acquaintance passes a rude remark about your child, or a parent of yours tells you about being mistreated by neighbors. As painful as these things are, they are minor offenses compared with the pain of loss that a parent feels when a child dies, or a depressed or defiant adolescent leaves home. They are also minor compared with the breakup of a marriage or the end of a long friendship.

Nevertheless, both large and small hurts are matters for forgiveness. The temptation to reserve the act of forgiveness for the major events of the cosmos is dangerous in that it allows for smaller hurts to go unattended and unhealed and to grow unchecked.

Remember that <u>forgiveness</u> reaches out and is <u>balm</u> for failures in all sizes.

forgiveness (cf) peace

5. Often, when someone else invites you into their lives to help them with their forgiving process, that person allows you the opportunity to look into your own life for places where you are not at peace and to work at restoring order in your own disarray.

The image of the wounded healer is apt here. The person who has experienced hurt and who has forgiven is the most trusted ally in aiding our efforts of forgiveness. That person could be you. On the other hand, the one who is not at peace with himself or herself is an unlikely mediator of peace for others.

6. Last, it may be helpful to keep in mind that being a peacemaker and a forgiver involves more than thinking good thoughts. It involves activity, not passivity.

Isaiah 2:4 tells us that God will adjudicate between many people and "these will hammer their swords into plowshares, their spears into sickles." The language is tough and muscular, like the effort of forgiveness itself. It is fair warning to all who are struggling with forgiveness to expect action and passionate involvement in the process.

TAKING INVENTORY

Too long have I lived
among people who hate peace,
who, when I propose peace,
are all for war.

Psalm 120:6–7

Opening a book like this has a way of catching us off guard and in the middle of things when it comes to forgiveness. There are places and people with whom we have buried the hatchet a long while ago. There are raw wounds that are currently so painful that we ache at a mere hint of their memories. There are some situations where we are in process, to one degree or another, of forgiving or of being forgiven.

Sometimes our own lives are peaceful and in harmony, but we are emotionally or geographically close to people who are struggling with forgiveness. In those situations, we may be asked to be a mediator of peace between two feuding parties, a harmonizer, a negotiator, a go-between.

This is time for taking stock of those situations, for taking inventory. On page 7 is a chart to help you do just that.

Think of situations in your personal life, in the lives of people known to you, and in the many communities in which you are personally involved (church, school, job, neighborhood, organizations) where forgiveness is or has been a factor. Big hurts or little hurts, past or present, deliberate or accidental—it doesn't matter— nor does the order in which you recall them. Write these in the column headed *Forgiveness Situations.*

D	FM	FS	C	O	X'	X⁵		FORGIVENESS SITUATIONS
							1	
							2	
							3	
							4	
							5	
							6	
							7	
							8	
							9	
							10	

On the left side of the numbers, use a check mark (✔) to indicate the status of these episodes or persons.

- Put a **D** if forgiveness is over and done with.
- Write **FM** if someone still needs to forgive you.
- Use **FS** if you still need to forgive someone (even if that someone is yourself).
- Use a **C** if the way is clear for forgiveness on your part, but the next step belongs to someone else.
- Use an **O** if you are placing an obstacle in the way of forgiveness.
- Look at where you put an O (obstacle). Put a check mark in the X^1 column for situations that have gone unforgiven for more than a year.
- Place a check mark in the X^5 column for situations that have gone unforgiven for more than five years.

Circle the situation that you would most like resolved.
Add to this list anytime you want.

PEACE:

Let It Begin with Me

Peace be with you.
John 20:20

The place to start is with ourselves. We will never be credible mediators of forgiveness and peace to others unless we have some very profound sense of peace within ourselves. Maybe that's why the first words spoken to his disciples by Jesus, the Prince of Peace, after his Resurrection were: "Peace be with you." It has to be with *you* before you can bring it to anyone else.

The Old Testament glimpses what it would look like to live in peace. It is a time when

> *The wolf lives with the lamb, the panther lies down with the kid,*
> *calf and lion cub feed together with a little boy to lead them.*
>
> *Isaiah 11:6*

Yet peace of an ordinary variety or the kind that surpasseth understanding is hard to come by—in your own life, in the lives of those you love, in your neighborhood, on your job, in the world around you.

If you take the peace greeting of Jesus as directed personally, then it is an invitation to harmonize your life and to synchronize your will with his. It is a time to take inventory and to expose to light any relationship—past or present—in need of healing and wholeness. It is the time to confront any obstacles that may stand in the way of breathing deeply the peace of Christ.

8

You may need some time to discover where you need to make peace with yourself, to identify places where peace is missing—to realize where you may need to forgive yourself.

Take time now to notice that:

- Peace is lacking in your life when _____

  _____ .

- There are disorder and disarray in your life with _____

  _____ .

- You need healing for _____

  _____ .

EXERCISE 3 INITIATING FORGIVENESS

If a (person) has received an injury, then even if the wrongdoer has not asked for forgiveness, the receiver of the injury must nevertheless ask God to show the wrongdoer compassion. . . .

The Talmud

In 1955 Martin Luther King, Jr., told his congregation at the Dexter Avenue Baptist Church in Montgomery, Alabama, during the lengthy bus boycott in that city, that peace and forgiveness rested in their hands. In *Strength to Love* King wrote:

> *. . . the forgiving act must always be initiated by the person who has been wronged, the victim of some great hurt, the recipient of some tortuous injustice, the absorber of some terrible act of oppression.*

Peace and forgiveness, therefore, rested with the Blacks whose houses were bombed, whose children were threatened, who themselves were beaten.

King insisted that forgiveness did not mean ignoring the evil that was done. It meant acknowledging evil for exactly what it was and, in the process, declaring that it would no longer stand in the way of a relationship. "Forgiveness," wrote King, "is a catalyst creating the atmosphere necessary for a fresh start and a new beginning."

There is a precedent for King's advice in the Gospel's command to

> *. . . go and be reconciled . . . and then come back and present your offering.*
>
> *Matt. 5:23–25*

As unreasonable as it seems, the Gospel suggests that the responsibility rests squarely with the person in Church, with the pray-er, with the believer, to take the first steps and to begin the forgiveness and reconciliation process.

10

Being a peacemaker cost Jesus his life. One way or another, it will cost us ours. "Go at once and make peace" is another way of saying, "Delay revenge." "Don't give your opponents a dose of their own medicine." "Go at once and put someone else's needs ahead of yours." That is always a way of dying a little.

The paradox of the process is that in this death there is a new life. In the long run, we extend new life to the one who offended us, new life to ourselves (who could have been swallowed and destroyed by hate) and new life to the relationship between us.

One question, then, is:

- Can you think of some places in your own life where you can take the first step and initiate the process of forgiveness?

And another question:

- Can you think of some places where you could encourage someone or some institution (your church, your government, some company or organization) to take the first step?

...in This Death there is A New Life

PRACTICING PEACE

> *Peace is not merely the absence of war. Nor can it be reduced*
> *solely to the maintenance of a balance of power between enemies.*
> *Nor is it brought about by dictatorship. Instead it is rightly and*
> *appropriately called an enterprise of justice.*
> "*Pastoral Constitution on the Church in the Modern World*,"
> *The Documents of Vatican II*

For everything there is a season. There is a time for arguing; there is a time for making up. There is a time for war; there is a time for peace. *And there is a time to practice peace!*

Imagine yourself as the chief peace negotiator in the following situations. In each case, record your peacemaking response.

THEY: "If she comes, we're not going."

SHE: "If they come, count me out."

YOU: _____

SHE: "Mom, he did it again."

HE: "No, I didn't."

SHE: "Yes, he did."

HE: "No, I didn't."

MOM: _____

THEY: "You're not going to invite her, are you?"

YOU: _____

COUNTRY A: "You broke the truce and attacked us!"

COUNTRY B: "You provoked us by stealing our supplies!"

YOU, THE PEACE AMBASSADOR: _____

THEY: "We can't have their kind in school."

"They're so dirty."

"And so noisy."

"They scare me."

YOU: _____

HE: "I'm sorry, but we have to leave the party."

YOU: "Do we have to go *now?*"

HE: "My office called. They need me."

YOU: _____

HE: "You're late."

SHE: "No, I'm not."

HE: "Yes, you are."

SHE: "No, I'm not."

HE: _____

1. What do all of these situations have in common?
2. When are unpeaceful situations the hardest to resolve?
3. Would it have been easier to "make war" than to "make peace" in these situations? Why or why not?
4. Which episodes reminded you of home base? How would these exchanges have been resolved there?

13

QUALITIES OF
A PEACEMAKER

How important for you are the following qualities of a peace-maker? Next to each put an **E** if you think it's essential; put an **NI** if you think it's not important; put an **FI** if you think it's fairly important; put an **H** if you think it's harmful. Be sure to add other qualities on the next page as they occur to you:

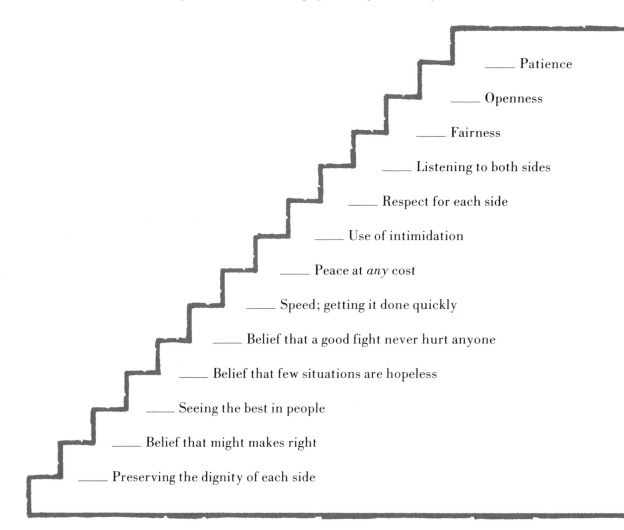

_____ Patience

_____ Openness

_____ Fairness

_____ Listening to both sides

_____ Respect for each side

_____ Use of intimidation

_____ Peace at _any_ cost

_____ Speed; getting it done quickly

_____ Belief that a good fight never hurt anyone

_____ Belief that few situations are hopeless

_____ Seeing the best in people

_____ Belief that might makes right

_____ Preserving the dignity of each side

For he is the peace between us, and has made the two
into one and broken the barrier. . . .

Ephesians 2:14

Any others?

_____ _____

_____ _____

_____ _____

_____ _____

_____ _____

_____ _____

Which ones are your strongest qualities? Go through the list
again and put an **S** (self) next to the ones that you own.

Here's another way to take inventory of your peacemaking qualities. Pretend you are the subject of a poll and have been asked to answer the following twenty questions. Circle **Y** (yes), **N** (no), or **M** (maybe). Skip those that you feel do not apply to you.

Are you a person who

1. will initiate forgiveness?   Y   N   M

2. demands an apology before you will grant forgiveness?   Y   N   M

3. frequently has a running feud going with someone?   Y   N   M

4. gossips, thereby starting arguments between people?   Y   N   M

5. thinks some deeds are unforgiveable?   Y   N   M

6. thinks it's harder for men to forgive?   Y   N   M

7. holds grudges?   Y   N   M

8. gets angry easily?   Y   N   M

9. loves a good fight?   Y   N   M

10. avoids conflict?   Y   N   M

11. believes in capital punishment?   Y   N   M

12. thinks admitting fault is for losers only?   Y   N   M

13. fakes reconciliations; pretends everything is O.K. when it isn't?   Y   N   M

14. provokes conflict?   Y   N   M

15. is merciful and compassionate?   Y   N   M

16. believes in an eye for an eye?   Y   N   M

17. believes only God forgives?   Y   N   M

18. has experienced being forgiven (by anyone)?   Y   N   M

19. thinks governments are strongest when they don't show mercy?   Y   N   M

20. equates strength with nonforgiveness?   Y   N   M

Now go back and look at your *maybes*. Be sure that each time you used a maybe you had no other choice and that it wasn't an excuse for evading a yes or a no answer.

Then, erase your answers or cover them over with a piece of paper, and ask someone you know to code and guess the answers that you made. You can learn something about yourself from the congruencies as well as the discrepancies in this sharing when it takes place in an open, caring atmosphere.

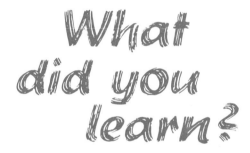

What did you learn?

EXERCISE 6 THE VOCABULARY OF FORGIVENESS

The quality of mercy . . .
It is an attribute to God himself;
And earthly power doth then show likest God's
When mercy seasons justice.

William Shakespeare,
The Merchant of Venice

Some words are life-giving. Some words are death-dealing. Forgiving words are restorative and hope-filled. Nonforgiving words are corrosive and terminal.

Take a look at the following exchange between one person who believed forgiveness and a new relationship were possible, and another person who believed the opposite:

I'm sorry.	*I'm not sorry.*
Let's make up.	*It will never be the same.*
There's still hope for us.	*It's hopeless.*
I didn't mean to hurt you.	*You don't deserve an apology.*
Let's be friends again.	*I don't need you.*
Let's forgive and forget.	*It's too hard to forgive you.*
Let's start over again.	*It won't work.*
I love you.	*Good-bye.*

The words you choose—the way you say them—how you go about it—they're all up to you. How would you rewrite the italicized unforgiving responses with peacemaking ones?

Or do you need words?

The father in Luke's Gospel (15:11–32) showed that he forgave his prodigal son in gestures. He *clasped* him in his arms (v. 20). He *kissed* him tenderly (v. 20). He *gave him gifts* (v. 22).

In another story (Luke 19:1–10), Zacchaeus was certain of God's forgiveness when Jesus *visited his house* (v. 7).

These gospel stories illustrate some ways of forgiving without words. Can you think of any others?

Steps in the Process of Forgiveness

Forgiveness is and always has been an impractical, illogical, and uncommon approach to life: forgiving our enemies, doing good to those who hurt us, repaying evil with kindness. Contrary to myth, forgiveness is not instinctive, and most of the time it is a very difficult and time-consuming enterprise.

Once in a while, we stumble across someone who has made forgiveness a style of life. Even for that person, it is not a question of forgiveness being easy, but more a matter of the truth and wisdom of forgiveness "hitting home." Thus, a person knows from experience that, as outrageous as it seems, forgiveness *is* the better way. That person is able to absorb a mind-set that allows forgiveness to be practice as well as theory.

There are no quick and easy access plans to that place where forgiveness is a life-style. There are, however, some tried-and-true *gradual* steps that we can keep in mind. These are stages that act as landmarks through the forgiveness process, stages that direct us, *eventually*, to freedom.

Some of those steps are:

- We love conditional acceptance -

Acceptance ← of the person as is

(1) **Acknowledge the hurt; affirm the pain.** This is not as obvious as it would seem. It frequently means swallowing your pride, admitting that you are hurt, admitting that someone or something got to you, admitting that you weren't as impervious to rudeness, thoughtlessness, criticism, rejection, neglect, ingratitude as you thought you were. And it means admitting that you are unable to snap out of it as quickly as those around you would like.

That's O.K.

It is far better to acknowledge the hurt and the pain than to put a bandage over an "infected spirit," an unhealed heart that might fester and rupture later.

Acknowledge the hurt—a necessary beginning.

(2) **Decide to forgive. Make an act of the will for the spirit to forgive.** In *The Will to Meaning*, Viktor Frankl tells us that he survived the depression, despair, and dehumanization of Auschwitz and Dachau by deciding that there was meaning in the suffering that he and others were enduring. He did not know *(nor might he ever know!)* what the meaning was, but making an act of the will that there was, that there *had to be meaning*, was a precious survival strategy.

intention

When it comes to forgiveness, you need not know *how* you are going to forgive. You need not determine a precise strategy or even see its actual possibility. All you need to do is decide that this is what you *will* to do. It helps. It is a step in the right direction.

(3) **Remember that forgiveness is a process and that it will take time.** When everyone around you is pushing for a quick reconciliation, remember that you are dealing with a hurt that, like a physical hurt, needs time to heal. This is discussed at greater length in Chapter 3, "Misunderstandings about Forgiveness."

20

4) **Remember that forgiveness isn't easy.** Some things that look like forgiveness (for example, the "martyr's" response: "It's O.K. with me that I always get the leftovers"; a phony reconciliation: "Didn't bother me a bit") look easy, but real forgiveness *always, always* involves a "little death" that is definitely not pleasant and easy to endure. There is more about this in the next chapter.

5) **Gather the testimonies and witnessings of people who have forgiven and listen to their experiences.** Find the stories that say to you: "I was there. I know how tough it is. I know what you're going through. I forgave, and so can you."

Replay their stories when needed.

This will prove to be invaluable encouragement when your own situation looks hopeless.

6) **Forgive yourself.** Sometimes, a double standard operates whereby others are treated more compassionately and are forgiven things for which we would never forgive ourselves. We wind up holding ourselves in bondage by not extending forgiveness to ourselves. Whatever it is that we have done—whatever mistake or failure or sin we have committed—it is only a part of who we are. We need to see that. We need to separate ourselves from our failure and to approve ourselves while disapproving the thing we did.

giving & receiving

We need to forgive ourselves because we will never be able to receive another's forgiveness, even God's, unless we do. I know a family of six brothers and sisters who forgave their oldest brother for mismanaging their inheritances. The oldest brother, a stockbroker who decided to take some risky chances in the hope of a bonanza, not only lost the bulk of their investment but also was not able to accept his siblings' forgiveness. He has not talked to any of them for a decade.

The point is that another's forgiveness can be real in your life only if you forgive yourself. If you are carrying a burden of guilt because you have not yet forgiven yourself, this may be the time to accept God's forgiveness and begin a new life!

7) **Try to see the one who hurt you in a new light.** Try to look at him or her as a person not free to love you, or possibly, not free to love anyone because of fear, prejudice, lack of education. isolation, insecurity, ignorance, unhealed hurts of the past.

acceptance of person as is...

Separate behaviors & person 'hate the sin' not the sinner

21

The one who Pursues Revenge should dig Two Graves

In the beginning of forgiving very painful hurts, this can be a distressing exercise, but *eventually* it becomes possible to see the one who hurt you as one in need of freedom—most probably more so than yourself. This is especially true of people who appear to be powerful and to have everything, but who are, in fact, in bondage to their destructive behavior patterns.

Remember when you were forgiven. Recall those times with gratitude when someone could have held something against you and did not. Be specific in this reflection—something forgiven at home when you were little, something forgiven at school, something you confided to another and he or she loved you anyway, someone who did not hold you in contempt for the thing you said or the thing you did. Remember how good you felt, how affirming it was, how you promised yourself or someone else that you would prove them right—that you really were as terrific as they believed!

Consider the consequences of nonforgiveness. A Chinese proverb puts it succinctly: "The one who pursues revenge should dig two graves." If you do not forgive, be prepared for the damaging consequences of nonforgiveness *to yourself!* A sobering reflection.

Pray. First, last, and always, the power to forgive comes from a place or person outside ourselves. In *The Hiding Place*, Corrie ten Boom tells the story of meeting the former SS man who had guarded the shower room at the concentration camp where she and her sister had been prisoners. The encounter happened after World War II. She had just lectured on forgiveness, and he thanked her for her message, extending his hand to shake hers. Her own hand was paralyzed as she recalled the ignominy of the camp, the death there of her cherished sister Betsie, and she prayed, "Jesus, I cannot forgive him. Give me your forgiveness."

Corrie ten Boom prayed and, as her hand, empowered from another Source, reached out to him, she learned that ". . . it is not on our forgiveness any more than on our goodness that the world's healing hinges, but on His. When he tells us to love our enemies, he gives, along with the command, the love itself."

An extraordinary testimony!

Celebrate it. Quietly, loudly, with loved ones, alone, find a way to mark the event of forgiveness, to honor the effort, to remember the grace, to commemorate peace.

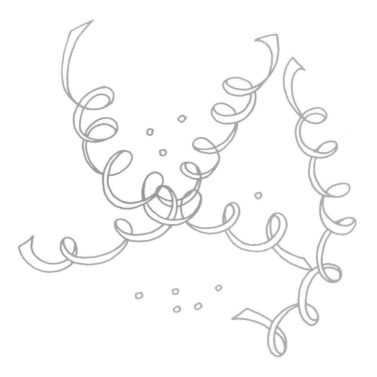

7 WILLING FORGIVENESS

> *Never repay evil with evil. . . . Do all you can to live at peace with everyone. . . . Resist evil and conquer it with good.*
>
> Romans 12:17–21

There is a story about a man who rides the bus to work each morning. Each day he is met by a sour, embittered bus driver who has only gruff words to offer his passengers.

"Why," a friend of the passenger asks, "do you put up with his rudeness? Why are you always so courteous and gracious when this man insists on insulting you?"

"Because," replies the passenger, "I refuse to let this man dictate to me how I'm going to act."

The point of the story is that this person *decided* (i.e., made an act of the will) not to be led by another's negative behavior, not to respond in kind but rather *to act freely*.

The truth buried underneath this story is a wise one to keep in mind when someone declines to praise you for a job well done, a friend forgets to invite you to a party, a spouse forgets your anniversary. Like the man in the story, we can refuse to be co-opted and to act in a similar way.

The title of this book refers to *practicing* forgiveness. One of the ways we can strengthen the practice of forgiveness is by willing it, by wanting it even when it appears impossible. Maintaining an *attitude* of forgiveness is a healthy step that prepares the ground for actually forgiving.

1. Are there some situations where forgiveness is needed and you don't have the strength to will it? Is there someone who could help motivate you to desire to forgive? Who?
2. Are there some situations where you are inclined (daily, weekly, monthly) to respond negatively because you are ill-treated and where you act as a free person? Where?

Rejoice and be glad, for your Reward will be great in Heaven

Matt. 5:12

EXERCISE *8* # MOTIVATING FORGIVENESS

Happy the merciful:
they shall have mercy shown them.
Matt. 5:7

We all need motivation to help us do things that are difficult. A vision of what you could look like in a bathing suit can encourage you to pass up dessert. The freedom from dependence on public transportation and the convenience of your own car could inspire you to study and pass a driver's examination.

So, too, we all need motivation for forgiveness, especially for those times when the alternatives to forgiveness are tempting. When you are able to say, although it is difficult, "I want to forgive," your motivation can be fortified by considering the following:

1. What nonforgiveness is doing *to you*; how it makes you a less pleasant person to be with; how it doesn't bring out the best in you; how it affects your self-esteem.
2. How destructive nonforgiveness is of relationships; how you try to manipulate your family and friends into "taking your side"; how preoccupied you are with your hurt that you find yourself enjoying your family and friends less.
3. How it depletes you of energy; how it consumes your thoughts; how it becomes a central drive and goal; how the whole effort of nonforgiving exhausts you.
4. How nonforgiveness affects your sleep; how many nightmares it has engendered; how even your unconscious has become involved in what you thought was only a conscious activity.
5. How it affects the good you do and the good you want to do by diverting your motives, by dividing you.

These are just samples of reasons why nonforgiveness isn't helping you. There are other reasons, too; feel free to add them to the list. You might spend some time reflecting on those items that are especially real to you and deciding what you plan to do about them.

9 **HOW OTHERS HAVE FORGIVEN**

I have given you an example so that you may copy what I have done to you.

John 13:15

The stories of people who have lived through great hurts and who have forgiven their enemies are very helpful witnessings for all of us.

One such story belongs to Graciella Martinez, a native of Cuba, who watched her thirteen-year-old son's execution in the early days of Castro's takeover of the island. His "crime" was that he was a newly evangelized believer, carrying a Bible and wearing a cross around his neck as witness to his faith in Jesus Christ. The punishment for this "dangerous" activity was death before a firing squad.

Graciella vowed revenge and devoted all of her time, energy, and money toward getting even with Castro and his regime for fifteen years following her son's death. Then, when she saw how destructive her hatred was *to herself and to the memory of her dear son*, she forgave.

Martin Luther King, Sr., forgave those responsible for the murder of his wife and those who killed his son.

The last words of Archbishop Oscar Romero of El Salvador as his bullet-riddled body slumped to the floor of the hospital chapel were, "God, have mercy on my assassins."

As he was being stoned to death, St. Stephen cried out, "Lord, do not hold this sin against them." (Acts 7:60)

From the Cross, Jesus said, "Father, forgive them; they do not know what they are doing." (Luke 23:34)

The Maryknoll community mourned the murder of two of their sisters in El Salvador, forgave, and promised not to abandon the poor and suffering people of that desperate country.

The witnessings of people who have forgiven extreme injustices can help me to

- forgive my neighbor's rudeness
- forgive my spouse's infidelity
- forgive my parents' mistakes
- forgive my children's ingratitude
- forgive unfairness where I work
- forgive a friend's betrayal
- forgive people who judge me falsely
- forgive a nation's injustice to the poor
- forgive a teacher's ineptitude
- forgive a church's indifference to the needy
- forgive myself my own failures and inadequacies
- forgive, possibly, *anything!*

And all because of the example of people who forgave more than I could ever imagine!

Some stories of people who have forgiven that have especially moved me are

_____

_____

_____

_____

These stories help us in another way. They remind us that forgiveness does not always mean turning the other cheek (Matt. 5:39). There are times when turning the other cheek is viewed not as a gesture of love, but as an act of arrogance and pomposity. There are other times when turning the other cheek is a convenient way to avoid involvement, and in those situations it is more harmful than helpful as a strategy.

The New Testament mentions turning the other cheek as one way to forgive. But it also offers a process for confronting (occasionally with witnesses) those who have wronged us (Matt. 18:15–18). All depends on the situation and the people involved.

While there is no sure-fire answer that applies across the board, there is one motivation that applies at all times, in every single instance, without qualification, and that is the goal to set someone free. Martin Luther King, Jr., explained that this strategy was the only way to "turn an enemy into a friend."

The point is twofold:

1. There is no single method that must be followed with regard to forgiveness.
2. Forgiveness does not abrogate our right, *our responsibility*, to work peacefully so that injustice does not repeat itself.

> *There have been intervals in which powerful individuals or nations have been able to cry "peace, peace" while injustice ravaged the lives of masses of people who paid the price for such surface peace (Jer. 6:14). . . . As God's people, we will not cry "Peace, peace" without the fullness of God's shalom.*
> *Peacemaking: The Believer's Calling*

10 # FORGIVING OURSELVES

> *"And anyway, punishment doesn't do a damn thing for the guilt, does it? It doesn't make it go away. And it doesn't earn forgiveness."*
> *"No," he says wearily.*
>
> from *Ordinary People* by
> Judith Guest

Once, the parents of a five-year-old boy forgave the woman responsible for seriously injuring their child in a car accident. The woman, a nurse on her way to work, said, "I'll never forgive myself." She never did.

The woman relived the accident hundreds of times in her mind. Over and over again, she told herself, "I'll never forgive myself for not being more careful, for not watching more closely, for not stopping sooner. I'll never forgive myself for not taking the bus."

The forgiveness offered by the parents of the little boy was never real to her. She was never able to accept it because she was never able to forgive herself.

When her husband said, "I love you. I know you meant no harm," she could not believe him.

When helpful neighbors and good friends made comments such as, "We know how loving you are. You are such a careful person. This was a terrible accident," she could not accept them.

The woman vowed that she would never drive again. She never did.

What happens to people who don't forgive themselves is more or less illustrated by this story.

People who don't forgive themselves

- *become depressed*, lose perspective, and let the negative event control their lives;
- *cannot be consoled* because they are unwilling or unable to let go of the past and start again;
- *experience guilt*. The Reverend William Sloane Coffin once said, "[Guilt] destroys us when, through repression, it mars our perception, and when, in our arrogance, we refuse forgiveness."
- *want to be punished* to settle the score, to "earn" forgiveness;
- *can't accept the forgiveness of others*. Obviously.

The point is that another's forgiveness can be real in my life only if I forgive myself. If you are carrying a burden of guilt because you have not yet forgiven yourself, this may be the time to accept God's forgiveness and begin a new life!

> *In other words, to accept forgiveness is to be made normal again, to be able to live the way we are supposed to live.*
> *William Sloane Coffin*

Forgiving ourselves is, ultimately, a matter of faith. Faith in the *power* of forgiveness. Faith in God's enduring love.

> *What God can compare with you:*
> *taking fault away,*
> *pardoning crime,*
> *not cherishing anger forever*
> *but delighting in showing mercy?*
> *Micah 7:18*

If you don't have that faith, you could pray for it, and you could ask others, especially those who "own" their faith, to join in that prayer with you.

If someone you know does not yet have that faith, you could pray that he or she be freed from torment and doubt and know a peace that surpasseth understanding.

...to accept Forgiveness is to be made Normal again...

31

EXERCISE *11* SIGNS OF FORGIVENESS AND PEACE

Lord, make me an instrument of your peace.
St. Francis of Assisi

There is no stereotype of peacemakers. They are as often men as women. They are tall, fat, short, thin—nurses, fathers, salespersons, executives, union organizers, actors, athletes, laborers, students, children, teachers, mothers.

Few take up peacemaking as their major career goal. St. Francis did. Francis wanted to be an instrument or a sign of peace so that people who came in contact with him would know what peace, pardon, and love were about.

Francis was right about signs. At various levels signs, symbols, signals, and sacraments express a reality so authentically that they participate in the reality itself. Francis was a genuine and transparent sign. His ego didn't get in the way of communicating forgiveness and peace.

Lord, make me an instrument of your peace.
Where there is hatred, let me sow love;
Where there is injury, pardon;
Where there is doubt, faith;
Where there is despair, hope;
Where there is darkness, light;
And where there is sadness, joy.
O Divine Master, grant that I may not so much
seek to be consoled as to console;
to be understood as to understand;
to be loved as to love.
For it is in giving that we receive;
it is in pardoning that we are pardoned;
it is in dying that we are born to eternal life.
St. Francis of Assisi

The "reality" about forgiveness that needs to be communicated in signs has to do with

wholeness	healing
peace	friendship
freedom	love
strength	conversion
unity	

Some "signs" that have participated in and communicated one or more aspects of the reality of forgiveness are

a handshake	a telephone call
a truce	a dove
a gift	an olive branch
a kiss	dinner with a former adversary

Some signs are more effective communicators than others. Which do you consider the most effective? How fully do each of these signs participate in the reality of forgiveness?

Which signs do you use?

CHAPTER 3

Misunderstandings about Forgiveness

Consciously and unconsciously, we are familiar with so many clichés connected with forgiveness ("forgive and forget," "forgive and regret") that setting aside a chapter to deal with some of them seems appropriate.

The fact of the matter is that forgiveness suffers from an image problem. It doesn't always look like what it is, and that basic inconsistency spawns a series of misunderstandings concerning some fundamental truths about forgiveness. For example, on the one hand there are those who believe that "good" people forgive easily and quickly, and that only ornery, crotchety people hold grudges and withhold forgiveness. "What's holding you up?" they wonder. "Forgive and get it over with."

On the other hand, there are those who consider people who forgive to be country bumpkins, dunces, and suckers. Forgivers are doormats, they say, always waiting to be stepped on by someone with more savvy and expertise in the ways of the world. To this second group, those who *don't* forgive are the wise, sophisticated, knowledgeable ones.

One of the reasons why it isn't easy to clarify these and other conflicting notions about forgiveness is that very little information is in circulation on the subject. In its absence, we are invited to cope with stress, to handle our guilt and anxieties, and to be reconciled as quickly as possible. I often think that we have been programed to bypass forgiveness and instead to move with haste from our hurts (step 1) to a reconciliation (step 3) that is often half-hearted and short-lived. Frequently enough, forgiveness (step 2) is ignored entirely in the healing process, which may account for the many shaky reconciliations that topple at the slightest ill wind.

It is sad that some people avoid forgiveness, and it's unfortunate that others regard it as the epitome of stupidity. But many others consider it honorable.

We all need to keep in mind the following principles about forgiveness.

1. **Forgiveness isn't easy.** It may look easy and we may have been taught it's a cinch, but the fact is that forgiveness involves a process that doesn't come naturally.

When the real effort of forgiveness takes place, there's nothing instinctive or, God knows, easy about it. Try forgiving a friend who has betrayed your confidence or a co-worker who tells lies about you.

Instinct urges us to pay back in kind: to be late for the next appointment if someone is late for this one; to take what is yours if you have taken what is mine.

Forgiveness isn't an instinctive response, such as ducking when a baseball is heading in your direction. The very first thing to realize is that forgiving involves a process that doesn't come naturally but must be learned. <u>Probably the surest indication that forgiveness is going on in your life is that there is a pervasive sense of difficulty surrounding the process.</u>

(2) **Forgiveness takes time.** Forgiveness is part of a process that begins with a hurt and ends, as its final and long-range goal, with the event of reconciliation. To reconcile means to bring together that which belongs together but which is apart; it works only when we pause to forgive, only when we become aware of the depths of the offense against us and the anger burning within us so that we can forgive with all our wits about us and ensure a lasting peace.

We do a great disservice to others and to ourselves (and especially to children for whom these habits last a lifetime) when we put time demands on forgiveness. Judgments that it "should" take only a weekend or a week or a year are unfair pressures placed arbitrarily on situations that call for their own inner-graced time frame.

We owe it to ourselves and to each other to recognize that the ability to forgive can't be rushed. We owe it to each other to offer time to confront our wounds, to face our hurts head-on, to vent our emotions. Only then can real healing begin.

(3) **Forgiveness doesn't mean forgetting.** The most popular misconception about forgiveness is that when we forgive, we forget. Most of the time we don't forget—and we aren't expected to.

The neglected parent who forgives his or her children is not asked to forget their ingratitude. <u>The goal is not to forget but rather not to let the children's negative behavior direct one's life and have it stand in the way of other relationships.</u>

Memories exert power in our conscious and unconscious lives. For this parent, it isn't the memory of the hurt that will lessen. What one hopes will lessen is the churning in the stomach or the pain in the arm or the headaches, as the *power* of the negative memory decreases.

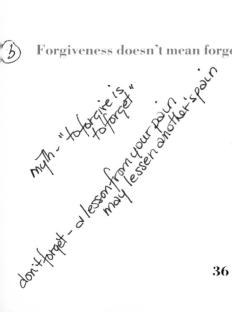

myth- "to forgive is to forget"

don't forget - a lesson from your pain may lessen another's pain

36

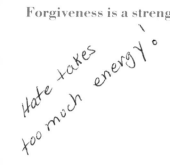

Forgiveness is a strength. It may look like a weakness and forgivers may look like dummies, but that's only because forgiveness suffers from an image problem. The fact is that forgivers refuse to be programed by those who are hurting them to retaliate and to hate back—which is precisely what a real enemy would want us to do. To break that cycle of violence by forgiving is a strength and a victory.

Hate never puts us in control. It does just the opposite. It puts us in bondage to someone else's evil deeds by counting on our bitter reactions to them. We wind up as prisoners to our enemy, who directs our behavior, our emotions, our life!

There is no particular strength in being towed around by someone else's fear, pride, ignorance, failure, or prejudice. In the long run—in the long run that sometimes looks as if it will never come—forgivers win.

Forgiveness has great benefits for you—the one doing it. Forgiveness is rarely motivated in its early stages by looking at the one hurting you and trying to see that person as a wonderful human being. In the beginning stages of forgiving, this strategy usually just doesn't work.

Initially, then, the best therapy is to consider what nonforgiveness is doing to *you:* how it affects your work, your self-esteem; how destructive it is of all your relationships.

Forgiveness reverses that destructive course of events. In other words, wrote the philosopher Hannah Arendt, "Forgiving . . . is the only reaction that does not merely react but acts anew and unexpectedly, unconditioned by the act that provoked it and therefore freeing from its consequences both the one who forgives and the one who is forgiven."

It is that freedom—*for the forgiver*—that is at stake here. Without forgiveness, both the doer *and the sufferer* are enclosed in a vicious cycle of vengeance capable of mutilating, if not destroying, each of them.

With forgiveness, hope, peace, love, and new life are possible for you.

EXERCISE *12* THE PRODIGAL SON

Read Luke 15:11–32

38

A young man received his share of money from his father and squandered it. Soon he was broke and wished he could change places with the pigs he was feeding. He decided to return home, hat-in-hand, willing to work as a servant in the home where he once was privileged. His father would not hear of this arrangement! Instead, he ordered a celebration that restored the son to his former status. The father was overjoyed at the homecoming.

The young man's brother was not as jubilant. Understandably so. He did not hug his brother. He did not weep tears at his homecoming. He did not attend the welcome-home party.

Maybe he said, "Wait a minute! Wait and give me *time* to forgive! I am unpracticed in the ways of forgiveness. My anger is fresh. My hands are still calloused from work he should have done and that I did for him in his absence. Where is justice? It is all so terribly unfair! I need time to sort things out. I'll forgive some day, but I don't want to fake a reconciliation until I mean it."

Are there places in your life where you have feigned or are now feigning a reconciliation? Code these episodes by using initials and list them here:

_____

_____

The father and the older brother teach us a lot about forgiveness. So does the younger brother. He was in a tough spot and he did something about it:

1. He made a plan.
2. He was willing to humble himself.
3. He followed through on his plan.

What could you do to free yourself from an unhappy situation? What could you do today?

EXERCISE *13* IDENTIFYING
MISUNDERSTANDINGS

Your next-door neighbor is the mother of a daughter or son who ran away from home at the age of thirteen. It is now two years later, and the parents have received word indirectly but through a reliable source that the daughter/son would like to come home.

The mother tells you how she loves her child, but how she doesn't want to look "soft" by forgiving too easily. Her husband agrees. They think they ought to play hard to get, give the child a tough time, teach her or him a lesson before they accept her or him back again.

The mother asks your opinion.

You say:

1. "You're the mother. You know best."

2. "Do whatever your husband says."

3. "Good idea! Don't let her [or him] forget the misery you went through."

4. "Your child is very brave wanting to try again. Do you think that a hard time from you might discourage her [or him]?"

5. "Why do you think (feel) you have to give your child a tough time?"

6. Something else?

Think about the misconceptions about forgiveness that might be guiding the mother (and possibly the father):

a. Forgiveness is supposed to be easy.

b. Forgiveness is a very quick process.

c. Forgiveness may make us look weak.

d. Forgiveness means forgetting how she [or he] hurt us.

e. Forgiveness has no benefits for us.

Think about your advice. Any misconceptions there?

THE APPEAL OF HATE

Hate usually seems to the hater to be so logical, so appropriate, so justified, that it is difficult for any healing power of love to interpose its neutralizing effect before some aggressive expression has occurred.

—*Karl Menninger, M.D.*

Hatred is like fire—it makes even light rubbish deadly.

—*George Eliot*

Hate is a prolonged form of suicide.

—*Johann Friedrich von Schiller*

Mindful that hate is an evil and a dangerous force, we too often think of what it does to the person hated. . . . But there is another side we must never overlook. Hate is just as injurious to the person who hates. Like an unchecked cancer, hate corrodes the personality and eats away its vital unity.

—*Martin Luther King, Jr.*

1. What are the essentials of what Menninger, Eliot, Schiller, and King are saying? Which did you find most convincing? Do you know why?

2. If you decide you agree with these quotations, what would that mean? Would there be any changes in your life? What changes?

Not to forgive is to save up grudges, to lick wounds, to resent (*re-sentire* = to feel again), to keep score of wrongs, to plot revenge, to remember the tiniest slight, to retaliate.

Not to forgive is to hate. It is to divert energy for the effort that hating commands.

Is it worth what hate is capable of doing to you?

Is it worth what hate *is* doing to you?

Martin Luther King, Jr., said it wasn't worth it.

What do you say?

15 WHY ASKING FOR FORGIVENESS IS DIFFICULT

Situations that involve the need for forgiveness are often messy and painful, so much so, in fact, that our resolve to forgive is often sidetracked.

Four of the most unpleasant aspects of forgiveness are

1. The hardest thing about forgiveness is *remembering*. Remembering the hurt . . . the people . . . the event(s) . . . the pain . . . the powerlessness. Reliving it all again!
2. The worst part of asking for forgiveness is admitting that I was wrong. It's *confessing guilt*, saying that I made a mistake!
3. Asking forgiveness is a *humiliation*. My pride and the image I have of myself have difficulty with asking someone's forgiveness. I'd much rather avoid the whole thing.
4. I am *afraid* that the person from whom I ask forgiveness will say, "No, I don't forgive you. You are an awful person who did an awful thing, and you don't deserve forgiveness."

FORGIV
REMEMBERING
FORGIV
AND HUMILIATIO

If *you* were to rank these deterrents in order of unpleasantness, which would come first? second? third? last?

1. _____

2. _____

3. _____

4. _____

Has any one of these unpleasantries stood in the way of your exercising forgiveness?

Does any one of these obstacles represent a reason why you are having trouble asking for forgiveness now?

EXERCISE **16** # WHY GRANTING FORGIVENESS IS DIFFICULT

Someone is in need of your forgiveness.

You are in the driver's seat. You are running the show. You have the upper hand. You are the one in control. You can either grant forgiveness or withhold it.

You feel the power of your position. Like a potentate, you can pardon if you care to. You juggle the options in your head. As you consider granting forgiveness, you become aware of some uncomfortable feelings inside you.

If you forgive,

1. You may look weak. No spine. No backbone. Where's all that anger you felt? Stir it up again and be strong against any temptation to forgive in the future.

2. You may be letting someone off the hook. Don't make it easy for him or for her. Extract every ounce that's due you. Demand that you be paid back in full.

3. You may have a responsibility to teach someone a lesson. Don't shirk it. Make it tough. Don't let the person who hurt you ever forget or live down what he or she has done. Remind him or her again and again. Tell everyone around that you just want justice to be done.

Are you withholding forgiveness now for any of these reasons? What can you do about it?

17 # THE CHAIN OF NONFORGIVENESS

Nonforgiveness has a way of involving or co-opting others into our strategy. For example, an ex-husband, angry at his former wife, might decide to "punish" his children living with her by not visiting them or not supporting them. He might try to align his parents (the children's grandparents), his brothers and sisters (the children's uncles and aunts), and mutual friends into his anger and resentments by insisting that they not communicate with the children either.

The emotions of nonforgiveness tend to lure as many persons as possible—some willingly and others indifferently—into an insidious web that hurts and polarizes.

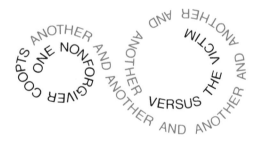

Even in situations such as these, forgiveness frees not only the one who forgives but also the network of persons from their supportive roles in the strenuous and dehumanizing effort of taking sides—*and forgiveness frees the victims as well!*

- Perhaps this is the time to consider the web that's been woven around a person who remains unforgiven . . .
- the time to look at the network of relationships affected:
- Who are the people pressured (subtly or not) into taking sides?
- Which are the relationships that have been strained?
- Which are the relationships that have been severely bruised?

CHAPTER 4

Obstacles
in the Way of
Forgiveness

Forgiveness isn't always a two-way street. Few things are more blessed than occasions when forgiveness is given and received, but those occasions are, sadly, rare. Often, we gather the courage to extend forgiveness only to find the other side unwilling, reluctant, or unable to cement a truce. With that in mind, let's consider five major obstacles that repeatedly hinder the act of forgiveness.

The person you need to forgive doesn't want to be reconciled. Let me give you a rather common and painful example. Let's say that you and a neighbor have been bickering for more than a year. You decide that it's time to bury the hatchet, but your neighbor is adamant about keeping up the feud. If you apologize, your neighbor angrily agrees that *you* are to blame and tells you that forgiveness is out of the question. If you extend forgiveness, your neighbor tells you that you have some nerve and slams the door in your face. It appears to be a no-win situation . . . until you remember that forgiveness doesn't have to be reciprocal to be real to you. Your sincere gesture toward peacemaking is a breakthrough that allows the dismantling of any walls that you have erected. It says that you are ready for peace. That is no small accomplishment.

Furthermore, when you forgive, your new behavior and your new attitude frequently speak more powerfully than words and eventually (not always, but often enough) crumble the other's hostility.

At the very least, you are left with the freedom of no longer holding a grudge or carrying a resentment. At most, you have taken the first steps toward reconciling a relationship—peacefully, genuinely, and reciprocally!

The person from whom you need forgiveness is withholding it. Again, so long as you are not obstructing the forgiveness process, you are doing all that you can. Remember that forgiveness takes time and that not everyone works on your timetable of readiness. Forgivers and those wanting forgiveness frequently get involved in a waiting game requiring patience and trust that the painful effort is worthwhile. For starters, you can feel relief by just tossing the ball into someone else's court. That gesture says that you are ready to make peace. You are then free to put the energies used for nursing grievances and licking your wounds elsewhere.

The person you need to forgive is dead. Last summer at a workshop I conducted in Nashville, a young man told me this story: Two months before, his father had died. The young man had only sketchy memories of his father, who had abandoned the family when the boy was six years old. The boy and his mother skimped and lived on the brink of poverty until the son could take on a job and support them both. Then, word came through distant acquaintances that the father had died. For fourteen consecutive nights after hearing that news, the young man had tortured dreams about his father until one night when the son said this prayer before he fell asleep:

> Dear Lord in heaven, my father is in pain. He is living in his death with a heavy burden of guilt for the hardship he inflicted on my mom and me. He wasn't much of a father, Lord, but I forgive him.
>
> Dad, I forgive you. It's O.K. Maybe you couldn't help what you did. I don't know, but I forgive you, Dad. I want you to rest in peace.

And the dreams about his father stopped that very night.

The power of suggestion? Catharsis? Who knows? I prefer believing that it all had something to do with the power of forgiveness because I have heard this kind of story repeated many times: forgiveness cutting through time and effecting reconciliations beyond the grave.

In similar fashion, I have witnessed very real forgiveness through a healing of the memories. As a process, the healing of the memories involves the willingness to touch base with painful past experiences in our lives so that these experiences will no longer haunt and threaten, but instead will be made whole. Dennis and Matthew Linn, S.J., appear to be wise and prudent guides to this process, and I recommend their book, *Healing Life's Hurts*, to those of you interested in pursuing this subject.

The person you need to forgive does the hurtful thing over and over again. A wife forgives her alcoholic husband for wasting a paycheck on liquor, for abusing her, and for frightening the children. He does the same thing the next week.

Why should she forgive again?

Here, I think it is not only necessary but also essential to keep in mind that:

a. Turning the other cheek is only one strategy with regard to forgiveness. Sometimes, a situation requires firmness in calling for an end to hurtful behavior. The wife in this example could forgive her husband and also demand that the negative behavior stop. She can even remain forgiving of him from a distance—at a home for battered wives, for example—until he gets his act together. Forgiving again and again doesn't mean putting yourself or someone else in danger. See Chapter 3, pages 36–37, and especially Exercise 9 for more on this.

b. Remember that some relationships demand an extra effort from us when it comes to forgiveness. We wouldn't be as concerned with working things out with a salesperson who continues to insult us as we would with harmonizing a relationship with a spouse or a parent or an employer who is a focal point in our career. Certain situations demand our efforts at forgiveness because the relationships represent a significant investment in our lives.

You need to forgive an institution, a society, an organization. Forgiveness applies to institutions as well as to people, and the process is the same. Institutions can inspire the same outrage, frustration, fury, and need for forgiveness that individual persons do because institutions are made up of people, some of whom are selfish, manipulative, unjust, cruel, thoughtless, rude, greedy, and unkind.

Seldom is forgiveness directed at a faceless institution. Try, and you will be able to see at least one human being behind the system. You may also be able to discern the fears and insecurities that helped to grease the wheels and allowed the unfairness, and maybe cruelty, to exist.

Looking at it another way, institutions, societies, churches, and governments that have a history of oppression could initiate the reconciliation process by asking forgiveness from those who have been hurt or offended by their predecessors. Even when this action is symbolic—for example, when forgiveness is asked of survivors of victims who are dead—it is a powerful and healing gesture.

EXERCISE *18* CALLED TO RECONCILE THE IMPOSSIBLE

Humpty Dumpty sat on a wall,
Humpty Dumpty had a great fall;
All the king's horses and all the king's men
Couldn't put Humpty Dumpty together again.

But maybe you can!

Maybe you were born to be a peacemaker, an *artisan de la paix*, as the *Jerusalem Bible* phrases it. . . .

Maybe you are called to be a mender, a reconciler, a bridge over troubled water.

Maybe you are just what a seemingly hopeless, desperate, and impossible situation needs to

 help someone sing a new song,
help someone see through winter to spring,
help someone want to begin again.

Is there a situation you know of where everyone seems to have despaired of the possibility of peace, and in which you feel called to be a peacemaker?

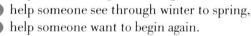 In your family?
In your neighborhood?
At work? At school?
In your church?
In your community? City? State? Nation?
 In the world?

Far-fetched? Not at all!

Betty Williams and Mairead Corrigan were two women from Northern Ireland who shared a dream and a hope that peace would come to that troubled country. Since they organized their Community of Peace People, violence in Northern Ireland has been cut in half. In 1976, their efforts were considered special enough for them to have been awarded the Nobel Prize for Peace.

Happy the peacemakers.

Matt. 5:9

Was there an occasion where you have helped make peace in what appeared to be a desperate situation?

No more wars, no more bloodshed. Peace unto you. Shalom. Shalom forever.

Menachem Begin

Peace is more precious than a piece of land.

Anwar el-Sadat

EXERCISE *19* PEOPLE WHO DON'T DESERVE FORGIVENESS

What are you thinking about, Jonah?
>*I'm being used again:*
>>*my message,*
>>*my style,*
>>*my way with words;*
>*Only this time I won't do it:*
>>*I'll be damned if I'm part of their salvation.*
>>*They don't deserve it,*
>>*They shouldn't be given a second chance,*
>>*They deserve to rot.*
>*What kind of God are you*
>>*that you will forgive even these people*
>>*if they turn to you?*

Jonah's hatred for the people of Nineveh was so intense that what he feared most was that they might listen to him if he were to preach to them and that, in turn, they would indeed repent and become friends of Yahweh. Fortunately for the Ninevites (and for himself), Jonah relented and preached Yahweh's message of repentance and forgiveness. It was with mixed emotions that Jonah lived to see every single Ninevite repent.

One of the emotions that Jonah wrestled with was jealousy—an emotion that does not let us rejoice with the good fortune of another. For Jonah, there was pain attached to seeing this contemptible group of people saved because of his ministerings.

Fortunately for the rest of us, Yahweh is not as myopic as Jonah. In His magnanimity, he claims that any *one* can be forgiven any *thing* provided he or she turns to Him with a contrite heart.

55

The only sign it will be given is the sign of the prophet Jonah.

Matt. 12:39

You might ask yourself: Are you more like Jonah or more like Yahweh when it comes to granting forgiveness?

Like Jonah, do you judge some persons and some groups as falling beyond the pale of forgiveness?	OR	Like Yahweh, do you grant unconditional forgiveness to all?
Like Jonah, do you feel resentment and jealousy when someone you deem unworthy is restored to a community, to a church, or to a family?	OR	Like Yahweh, do you rejoice and bless the homecoming of everyone?
Like Jonah, do you try to work against reconciliations?	OR	Like Yahweh, are you a peacemaker and mediator of reconciliations?
Like Jonah, do you withhold mercy?	OR	Like Yahweh, do you extend mercy to all, even to those hardest of all to forgive?

Take a piece of paper and jot down the names or initials of those persons you feel do not deserve forgiveness.

Is your reason the same as Jonah's? If it is, write a **J** next to each name. As best as you are able to sort out, is your reason Resentment?—Put an **R.** Anger?—Write an **A.**

Something else? Be specific and label your reason.

EXERCISE *20* FORGIVING GOD

God, sometimes I wonder
   why you didn't make me different:
   why I'm not smarter,
     or better looking,
     or more creative, compassionate,
   independent, obedient, assertive, talented, coordi-
   nated—or whatever I'm not that I would like to be.

Everything—absolutely everything—is under your control.
Who, but you, is responsible?
Whom, but you, do I have to blame?
Whom, but you, do I have to forgive?

God, sometimes I wonder
   why you have allowed me to make the mistakes I
   have made,
     why you didn't stop me,
     why you didn't interfere,
     why, when I failed or succeeded, you let me
   miss the point entirely.

58

Everything is under your control.
Who, but you, is responsible?
Whom, but you, do I have to blame?
Whom, but you, do I have to forgive?

> God, sometimes I wonder
>> why my enemies are doing so well,
>> why you let them laugh at my misfortune and misery,
>> why things didn't work out differently.

> God, I do not understand why you have not done
>> things as I would have done them.
>>> But I believe,
>>> *I want to believe*,
>>> that there is a purpose, your divine and holy purpose, behind these events, and that even if I do not understand I can pray, "May your will be done."

> Forgive *me*, God, for looking at what is not and
>> for not appreciating what *is*.
> Forgive me for romanticizing.
> Forgive me for living in unreal worlds.
> Forgive me for not taking responsibility for
>> changing things.
> Forgive me for settling for less than your plan
>> that I glimpsed often enough through your grace.

>> Amen.

> Forgiving God.
> Sometimes there is need for precisely that. Is there a need for *you* to forgive God? If so, what do you plan to do about it? What do you plan to do about it today?

21 Putting Yourself in
Someone Else's Shoes:
CONFLICT WITH A PARENT

(The actual difficulty involved in putting forgiveness into practice lies halfway between how simple it looks when you are reading about it in a book and how impossible it appears when you've been deeply hurt by someone.

The following exercise may help bridge theory and practice by inviting you to consider a situation where forgiveness is needed. See what you make of it.)

Assume you are a young man or woman who has recently moved away from home into your own apartment. You have a dinner party for some friends and your parents.

After a while the conversation turns to cooking skills—yours. Your mother has a few choice tales to relate about your ineptitude in the kitchen. You feel like crawling under the table, but your mother isn't finished. After your cooking has been dissected, your mother entertains the rest of your company with stories about your driving, your lack of organization, your clumsiness, and the difficulties you have handling your finances.

You've been through this with your mother before. You've told her you don't appreciate her critical comments, always given in public, and that you'd wish she'd stop. Your mother tells you that no one seemed to mind and that you're just too touchy.

Your father suffers through this embarrassing episode with you, takes you aside before they both leave, and says: "Be gentle with your mom; she doesn't mean any harm."

"But, Dad, this is the fourth time in three months. How much can I take? Enough is enough!"

Why should you forgive again?

1. Think through the following options and consider the advantages and disadvantages of each.

    a. Because she's your mother, and that's enough reason.

       Advantages _____

       Disadvantages _____

    b. Because you feel sorry for her.

       Advantages _____

       Disadvantages _____

    c. Because your dad asked you to.

       Advantages _____

       Disadvantages _____

    d. Because if you and she get into a big tiff, she may escalate the argument and cut you out of her will.

       Advantages _____

       Disadvantages _____

    e. Because your mom probably has unhealed hurts of her own, and probably doesn't know how to tell you she loves you, or at least doesn't know how to converse intimately with you. And because you have enough insight to see through these things, and enough faith to support you, you can expand the context of the situation and love her in return.

       Advantages _____

       Disadvantages _____

    f. Some other reason, such as _____ .

       Advantages _____

       Disadvantages _____

2. Some relationships are worth our trying harder to forgive and be reconciled. Is this one of those relationships? Why or why not?

3. Can you think of some strategies for forgiveness other than turning the other cheek that might apply in this situation?

4. Is there a way that the father in this story could be an effective mediator of peace? Is there a way that he is part of the problem?

22 Putting Yourself in Someone Else's Shoes: THE PAIN OF DIVORCE

(Here is another exercise to help you gain some facility in putting forgiveness into practice. It works best when you share your approach and style with someone else, preferably with someone who understands something of the gift that forgiveness is.)

Your brother and sister-in-law have recently been divorced.

Your brother is angry, hurt, resentful. His former wife extracted a large financial settlement, married his best friend, and she moved more than two thousand miles away with an adored five-year-old son.

You notice that your brother doesn't look very well. In addition, he's edgy, he's lost weight, you think he drinks too much, he's lost his appetite, and he's admitted that he isn't sleeping very well.

He tells you he feels like a failure.

He tells you he'll never forgive his former spouse for her deceit, her unfaithfulness, for how she ruined his life.

1. You say

   a. Nothing. After all, you're not a professional psychiatrist.
   b. That you agree with him. He *is* a failure. His life *is* hopeless.
   c. "I don't know what to say."
   d. "Chin up! It's not as bad as you think it is."
   e. Something hopeful, such as ———————————————— .

2. You have read a bit on forgiveness. You know some misconceptions, some stages, some obstacles. Is any of that information applicable here?

   Which? ——————————————————————————————

   Where? ——————————————————————————————

3. Think through the assistance you offered in this hypothetical situation. Was it free from misconceptions about forgiveness? Did it help dismantle any obstacles?

   Which ones? —————————————————————————————

   ——————————————————————————————————————

   You may have just provided some very valuable assistance on the subject of forgiveness. Perhaps you may now be encouraged to take one of your own forgiveness needs to an objective person for advice.

   While you're thinking about it, jot down the names or initials of someone who could be of just this kind of help to you.

CHAPTER **5**

God's Forgiveness

"To err is human; to forgive, divine" must mean that God has something to say about forgiveness.

God does.

Both the Old and New Testaments remind us that God manifested many supernatural qualities—none grander or more appreciated than the power to forgive.

There is uncertainty in the Old Testament about the derivation of the words "forgive," "remit," and "pardon," designated by the Hebrew word *salach*. Some say it has roots in the Accadian *salāhu*, which means "to sprinkle." In Accadian medical literature, the word *salāhu* is connected with a sprinkling of water or oil or another therapeutic liquid, and that motif would be compatible with the Hebrew understanding of the relation between forgiveness and healing.

In the Old Testament In addition to using the abstract term "forgive," the Old Testament writers presented some vivid descriptions of what occurred in the process of God's forgiveness. For the most part, these descriptions of forgiveness accompanied a parallel notion of sin:

I am indebted in this section to the work of William Klassen, *The Forgiving Community* (Philadelphia: Westminster Press, 1966).

65

When sin was depicted as a disease or a sickness,

> *(There is) no soundness in my flesh . . . no health in my bones,*
> *because of my sin.*
>
> Psalm 38:3

then Yahweh's forgiveness was connected with wholeness:

> *Cure me, for I have sinned against you.*
>
> Psalm 41:4

When sin was pictured as a burden, a weight, a power that restricted freedom, Yahweh's forgiveness could:

> *Instill some joy and gladness into me, let the bones you have crushed*
> *rejoice again.*
>
> Psalm 51:8

When sin was portrayed as a stain, Yahweh's forgiving action was depicted as cleansing:

> *Though your sins are like scarlet,*
> *they shall be as white as snow;*
> *though they are red as crimson,*
> *they shall be like wool.*
>
> Isaiah 1:18

When sin was presented as something from which the sinner could not be separated, Yahweh's forgiveness was portrayed with might:

> *He takes our sins farther away than the east is from the west.*
>
> Psalm 103:12

In the
New Testament The New Testament introduced John the Baptist who preached a baptism for the forgiveness of sins (Luke 3:3). He was forerunner to Jesus, who dealt directly with sinners (apart from the use of parables and other teachings on the subject) on six separate occasions. When we review those episodes, we find that

When Jesus healed the paralytic and said, "My child, your sins are forgiven," he scandalized the Jews present, who were accustomed to hearing the rabbis teach a collective forgiveness of sin but had never before witnessed someone personally conferring forgiveness on another individual. "How can this man talk like that? . . . Who can forgive sins but God?" was a question of out-and-out astonishment. (*Cf.* Mark 2:1–12 and parallels.)

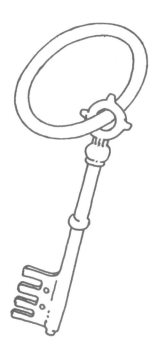

When Jesus forgave the woman at Simon's house, he was able to separate her from her past, her reputation, and her sin by "owning" the person and "disowning" the sin—a pattern of reconciliation that has been part of the Church since then. (*Cf.* Luke 7:36–50.)

Jesus dealt with Peter's confession, "Leave me, Lord; I am a sinful man" (Luke 5:8), by leaving Peter the binding and loosing responsibility signified through the keys (Matt. 16:18–19; 18:15–18), thereby suggesting that this power—and power it is—rests in the hands of sinful persons who are able to admit who Christ is (Luke 9:20) and confess and weep over their sins (Luke 22:62).

When Jesus ministered to the woman taken in adultery who had been presented to him to test his knowledge of the Law, he "unglued" her from her sin *and* "glued" the accusers to theirs in order to render them capable of repentance (John 8:1–11).

Jesus dealt with Zacchaeus by singling him out (not, as one might expect, the other way around) and by visiting him at his home. Maybe this means that we need not wait for the person who needs our forgiveness to come to us, but instead we could initiate the process. (*Cf.* Luke 19:1–10.)

When Jesus forgave the thief on the cross (*Cf.* Luke 23:39–43), we know that his first major miracle with the paralytic and his last with the thief involved forgiveness. That may be a clue to the importance of this theme and this ministry for Jesus and the early Christian community.

A Theology of Forgiveness   In both the Old and the New Testaments, there is a similar theology of forgiveness with respect to the following:

God's forgiveness is a gift. We don't earn it; we don't deserve it. It is a totally free offer whereby God loves us, accepts us, and marks our debts "paid" and our accounts "settled."

You are forgiven! Right now, without bargaining, groveling, getting dressed up, doing anything to merit it, or even asking for it, *you are forgiven!* The only thing left is to make God's forgiveness *real* in your life by *accepting* it.

God's forgiveness involves repentance. Accepting God's forgiveness involves repentance that directs ✱✱✱ us to seek the "realignment" of our destructive energies in more constructive ways. Repentance is the very appropriate response to God's

... repentance an appropriate response to God's forgiveness ...

repentance is thank you note for God's forgiveness

initiative of forgiving love. It does not merit forgiveness for us but rather allows us to accept forgiveness that is being offered.

God's forgiveness involves confession. Confession of our sins brings to light what was hidden. Dietrich Bonhoeffer wrote that "the expressed, acknowledged sin has lost its power because it has been revealed and judged as sin."

Confession is another appropriate response to God's forgiveness. It is a way to surrender what it is that separates us from God and each other and, according to Bonhoeffer, "to stand again in the fellowship of sinners who live by the grace of God in the Cross of Jesus Christ."

God's forgiveness is powerful. "What god can compare with you," the prophet Micah asks, "taking fault away, pardoning crime . . . ? Once more have pity on us, tread down our faults, to the bottom of the sea throw all our sins" (Micah 7:18–19). Who are you indeed, who is able to prove to us that because of your forgiveness there is no event of human life, even those that turn out badly, that is beyond repair? That is precisely what the radical event of forgiveness instructs.

. . . we are not irretrievable . . .

God's forgiveness is ours to share. Forgiveness cannot be simply received and treasured. It must, to remain active, be mediated to others. As a point of fact, the parable of the two debtors tells us that if we don't share forgiveness, we probably didn't receive it, appropriate it, and make it our own in the first place.

23 **TESTING FOR TRUTH**

If we say we have no sin in us, we are . . . refusing to admit the truth.

1 John 1:8

The choice for John was simple: admit your sinfulness and face reality, or deny your sinfulness and avoid reality. There is hope for us with the truth because

. . . if we acknowledge our sins, then God who is faithful and just will forgive our sins.

1 John 1:9

What it boils down to is this: Don't fool yourself. Don't pretend to be O.K., whole and healed, and living in the sunshine with a rainbow over your shoulder when in truth you are broken, vulnerable, imperfect, sinful, incomplete, and frequently living in darkness.

John encourages what psychiatrists would call a grounding in reality. To live in reality is to know myself, especially to know myself as a sinner, and most especially to know myself as a forgiven sinner. The inner honesty that prompts that self-disclosure clarifies my identity and lets me live in the bright light.

To acknowledge myself as a sinner, even a forgiven one, is not as easy as you might think. In *Life Together*, Dietrich Bonhoeffer laments:

> The final breakthrough to fellowship does not occur because, though they have fellowship with one another as believers and as devout people, they do not have fellowship as the undevout, as sinners. The pious fellowship permits no one to be a sinner. So everybody must conceal his [her] sin from himself [herself] and from the fellowship. We dare not be sinners. Many Christians are unthinkably horrified when a real sinner is suddenly discovered among the righteous. So we remain alone with our sin, living in lies and hypocrisy. . . .

These antithetical themes of darkness and light, reality and unreality, hypocrisy and truth, give us some things to think about:

1. To begin with, the critical question might be: How well do you know your sinful self?

_____

   Well enough to admit your sinfulness to yourself in particular rather than in vague terms?

_____

   Well enough to confess your sins to God?

_____

2. Do you know someone—at least one person—with whom you can share your own doubts, failures, mistakes, and sins?

_____

   Do you do this on a regular basis? If not, would there be an advantage for you in that kind of sharing?

_____

3. Are there persons who invite that disclosure from you whom you rebuff? Why do you suppose that is so?

_____

4. Do you provide an atmosphere of openness, honesty, acceptance, and light that allows others to admit their failings and sinfulness— or do you put pressure on others to cover up and pretend?

_____

WE REMAIN ALONE

WITH OUR SIN

EXERCISE *24* SHARING FORGIVENESS

*Were you not bound, then, to have pity on your fellow
servant just as I had pity on you.*

Matt. 18:33

A servant owed his master a huge sum of money, but he could
not repay him. Desperate, the servant pleaded for patience and begged
for mercy. Moved with pity, the master forgave the debt.

The freed servant quickly pounced upon a fellow servant and
demanded a mere pittance owed him. The fellow servant pleaded for
patience and begged for mercy. But the forgiven servant wouldn't
budge. Instead, he had the fellow servant thrown into jail.

When the master heard this, he was very angry, rescinded his
forgiveness, and had the servant thrown into jail until he could repay
the debt.

Jesus said of this parable:

*And that is how my heavenly Father will deal with you unless you
each forgive your brother (sister) from your heart.*

Matt. 18:35

Similar sayings are found elsewhere in the New Testament:

And when you stand in prayer, forgive whatever you have against anybody, so that your Father in heaven may forgive your failings too.
                                                        Mark 11:25

And forgive us our debts, as we have forgiven those who are in debt to us.
                                                        Matt. 6:12

Yes, if you forgive others their failings, your heavenly Father will forgive you yours; but if you do not forgive others, your Father will not forgive your failings either.
                                                        Matt. 6:14–15

And forgive us our sins, for we ourselves forgive each one who is in debt to us.
                                                        Luke 11:3–4

The theme of the parable of the two debtors (Matt. 18:23–35) carries through the theme of the petition of the Lord's Prayer that asks God to "forgive us our debts, as we have forgiven those who are in debt to us." In addition, the parable gives us an example of what it looks like when God forgives and we don't, and it shows us what God does about it. It is an ominous story!

The repetitive presence of sayings in the Gospels indicating a connection between God's forgiveness and ours reminds us that:

1. Forgiveness is not something that God alone declares. It is an activity we all are called upon to share with one another.

2. Forgiveness is not passive receptivity. When we receive forgiveness, there is an outreach activity that prompts us to extend it to others.

3. Forgiveness is a gift. We don't earn it.

4. One of the marks of the community of the Church is that it is a place where forgiving neighbors can exist side by side in peace.

Any departure from or infraction of these truths is dealt with severely, as the parable of the two debtors illustrates. That parable asks us all to put ourselves in the presence of the forgiving Lord and to consider

Unfair demands we place on one another. Like the unmerciful servant, are there places in our lives where we are unreasonably demanding of someone? Are there places where you need to loosen your grip? Your expectations? Your demands? Are there places in your life where people are suffering because of you and your unforgiving attitude?

Inconsistencies in our lives regarding forgiveness. Like the servant, do we ask for mercy for ourselves and refuse to grant it when it is asked of us? Is there an inconsistency in your own life in this regard—a place where kindness and favor were bestowed upon you and where you did not share it with others? Is there a double standard operating in your life that allows you to forgive the faults of acquaintances and not those of your family? Think about that. If it's true, what do you plan to do about it?

73

25 WHERE WE NEED FORGIVENESS

If we translate the official names of the cardinal sins into their approximate equivalents in modern speech, they begin to sparkle with relevance.

—*Karl Menninger, M.D.*

One of the chapters in Dr. Karl Menninger's successful and chastening book *Whatever Became of Sin?* is called "The Old Seven Deadly Sins (and Some New Ones)."

For those among us who need our memories refreshed as to the names of the "old" seven deadly sins, they are envy, anger, pride, sloth, avarice, gluttony, and lust.

Dr. Menninger invites us to consider new understandings of "old" forms of sin and to reflect on some deeds that qualify as contemporary deadly sins. For example, for

Pride Think about vanity, egocentricity, arrogance, self-adoration, self-ishness, even self-deification.

Sins of Sensuality Think about pornography, loveless intercourse within marriage.

Sins of Gluttony — Think about foods, drinks, drugs; rethink cravings for liquor, tobacco, caffeine.

Sins of Anger, Violence, Aggression — Rethink counter-violence, especially of the official kind (e.g., Attica prison), rethink ill humor, sharp words, denunciation or destructive criticism, glares, curses, rudeness, ingratitude.

Sloth — Think about inactivity, unresponsiveness, the "fear of becoming involved," apathy, laziness, callousness.

Envy — Think about the need to possess, to possess as one's "own" what belongs to someone else. After all, envy is "the sister of greed and a half sister of stealing."

Greed — The "rodent propensity" of grasping, seizing, taking, stuffing away.

So much for the "old" seven deadly sins. But there are more. Dr. Menninger says there are some new forms of sin just as lethal and destructive to community as the old ones. See if you can follow through Dr. Menninger's list by concretizing these "new" forms of deadly sins with specific examples of where they are happening in the world (and where they may be happening in your own life):

Sins of Affluence Think about the pileup work ethic versus the "small is beautiful" and the "theology of enough" proposed by E. F. Schumacher.

For example _____

_____

Sins of Waste Think about possessions causing pollution; wasting the lives of people confined to ghettos and slums.

For example _____

_____

Sins of Cheating and Stealing Think about cheating the American Indians and the appropriation of their lands; think about pilfering from employers.

For example _____

_____

Sins of Lying Think about maneuvering, manipulating, and misrepresenting facts; think of how governments do it.

For example _____

_____

Cruelty as a Form of Sin

to Children Think of the epidemic rise of child abuse.

to Animals Think of the slow death of birds and animals in the crates and bins of so-called roadside zoos.

Psychological Cruelty Think of name-calling, defamation of character.

For example _____

_____

Now think of *undoing* the examples of the new deadly sins. How could you and the community around you go about it?

26 REVIEWING THE GOOD WE DID NOT DO

Each of the seven deadly sins (pride, envy, anger, sloth, avarice, gluttony, and lust), with the exception of sloth, is a *sin of commission*, which means that it involves our *doing* something.

Yet sometimes we sin *by not doing something*. At these times, we are responsible for *sins of omission*.

Write the opposite next to each of the seven deadly sins. For example, the opposite of sloth is workaholism, and the opposite of lust might be frigidity. See how well you do with the remaining five deadly sins in pinpointing their opposing flaws.

(dull, sluggish)
(not flagging in zeal)

sloth —— workaholism / addiction

(strong desire of any kind)
(evil if inconsistent w/ the will of God

lust —— frigidity / complacency

(puffed up - boast; vainglory)

pride · vanity   self-denying; self flagellating

(envy desires to deprive another)   (feeling of displeasure at another's good fortune)

envy   pleasure in another's misfortune (contentment)

(indignation, vengeance, wrath)

anger   apathy, ignoring

(inordinate desire for wealth)

avarice   not caring for things we do have
taking things for granted

(belly -)

gluttony ——   impoverishment
paralyzed frozen

too much of anything   anger

78

With the exception of sloth, all the opposites are sins of omission. In sloth's case, the opposite (being a workaholic) is both a sin of omission and one of commission. Can you explain that?

_____

_____

Can you also illustrate each of the sins of omission with a concrete example from daily life?

Sins of Omission   *Example*

_____   ___   _____

_____   ___   _____

_____   ___   _____

_____   ___   _____

_____   ___   _____

_____   ___   _____

_____   ___   _____

EXERCISE *27* FREEDOM

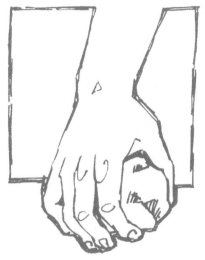

"Neither do I condemn you," said Jesus.
John 8:11

An execution was at hand. A woman caught in the act of adultery was presented to Jesus to test his knowledge of and fidelity to the Law. It appeared to be something of a no-win situation for Jesus. If he chose to free the woman, he disobeyed the law that claimed her life as punishment for her deed. If he condemned her, his reputation as a compassionate teacher was compromised.

Her accusers presented the woman to Jesus not as a penitent but as a condemned person, glued to her sin and totally identified with it. The woman herself made no plea for forgiveness, yet Jesus offered nothing else. The strength of forgiveness had the power to separate her from her sin, to give her new life, to confer self-respect, to help her see her own worth. Jesus refused to judge her as others did. He didn't punish her. Instead, he gave her freedom.

1. The woman in this story was used and exploited by men. Many women are, and you may know some of them. Will you offer a liberating word to one of them this week?

   Speaking of words, is your vocabulary free from sexist prejudices and style? If it is, are you forgiving of those whose language is not?

2. The woman in this story was guilty of charges brought against her. There are many persons—men, women, and children—who have been accused of charges that are false. Some of these people are not only accused but also are suffering and being tortured right now in prisons in many parts of the world.

Amnesty International works on behalf of these forgotten prisoners by writing letters that put pressure on authorities who can do something.

In 1977, Amnesty International was awarded the Nobel Prize for Peace. You can be part of their letter writing and peacemaking effort. To get started, contact:

Amnesty International U.S.A.
304 West 58th Street
New York, New York 10019

TEL: 212/582-4440

Epilogue

Thirty years ago, a seven-year-old boy was riding between his two older brothers in the backseat of the family car. Suddenly, their mother, drained and distraught from the experience of her husband's abandonment and a recent divorce, reached over the front seat and slammed the seven-year-old across the face with her hand. "You! The only reason I had you," she screamed, "was to keep your father. I never wanted you! I hate you!"

The scene was indelibly engraved in the child's memory. Over the years, the mother reinforced the sincerity of those remarks by praising the older sons and by unnecessarily and continually finding fault and blame in the youngest one. The youngest faithfully sought the mother's approval and blessing, but it never came.

Years later, the depth of his resentment, hurt, and anger became clearer. For years, it was he who remained devoted to his mother, cared for her, did the many chores around the house willingly and lovingly only to be rejected at every turn. He wondered if he could ever forgive her. He knew he wanted to try because the resentment and hurt he felt gnawed at him relentlessly and he found himself emotionally imprisoned.

I saw the son many months after he made his decision to forgive. "I can't tell you how many times in the last twenty-three years I relived the scene as a boy in the car," he told me. "Thousands, probably. But recently, while I was reliving it, I put myself in my mother's place for a change. Here she was, a high school graduate with no money, no job and a family of four to support. I realized how powerless, lonely, hurt, and depressed she must have felt. I thought of the anger, the fear, the pain that must have been there. And I thought of how much I must have reminded her of the failure of all her young hopes. It was the beginning of my forgiveness of her."

"I debated," he continued, "whether to tell her any of this. I prayed. My forgiveness deepened and so did my desire to talk with her about this, and I finally did. I was not sure I could find the right words, and above all, I did not want her to feel guilty. I told her that I understood and that I loved her. We wept in each other's arms for what seemed like hours. It was the beginning of a new life for me. For *us*."

At the end of this book, the most important truth that I can leave you with is that forgiveness is always the beginning of a new life for you. That promise of a new beginning makes forgiveness the linchpin in all relationships where a disjointing has taken place. In families, in communities, even among nations, forgiveness is the glue that cements peace and just living for us all.

Program
for
Youth/Adult
Education

to accompany
Putting Forgiveness
into Practice

General Introduction   The purpose of this educational outline is to provide a procedure for working through *Putting Forgiveness into Practice* with a group of adults for five weeks. Each of the five chapters in the book lends itself to an independent work unit.

Adults will relate to the material in this book without any difficulty and usually with great enthusiasm. As a facilitator, teacher, guide, or group leader, it may be helpful for you to recognize that

1. Every adult member of your group is currently involved in some phase of the forgiving process—either as needing to grant it or to receive it personally or as a go-between in family, neighborhood, or work situations. The following programing will help you to open the subject so that individuals can see where they stand in relationship to it.
2. Discussion will be most profitable if it is not limited to the "theory" of forgiveness. It will be up to you to maintain a climate that respects the personal revelations made by members of your group and that encourages honest and open discussion.
3. After you and your group or class discuss the points made in the introduction to each chapter, feel free to alternate the use of the exercises. These can be done alone, in small groups, or with the participants assembled together. Still other exercises might be done at home. Some lend themselves to private reflection; others, to group discussion. Use your imagination and sensitivity to the group and its needs. The procedural plan that will follow shortly is only a suggestion; please adapt it as you see fit.

The book can be used

- *in adult-education programs.*
- *in high school/college courses.*
- *with special support groups* of persons who have experienced (or are close to persons with) great hurts.
- *personally by individuals.* Your familiarity with the material covered in the book will help in advising it appropriately to others.
- *in self-discovery/personal-awareness programs* as a resource for identifying unforgiven hurts that stand in the way of personal growth. It is also an effective vehicle for learning techniques in interpersonal relations through the strength of forgiveness.
- *in social-justice courses* as a means of raising consciousness with regard to social and human rights, and justice issues that connect with forgiveness and peace.
- *in a course on forgiveness and reconciliation in a religion curriculum* or as part of a course complementing curricula in religion programs and courses. See Bibliography for suggested further readings.
- *in parish renewal programs* as reading and exercise material.
- *in sacramental preparation classes* that involve parents and other adults, especially in connection with First Penance/Reconciliation. (See Supplement: *Sacramental Program* after fifth-week program.)

Once again, these are only suggested places where the book can be applied. When you keep your eyes and ears open to needs that this book addresses, you may come up with other opportunities for using it creatively.

87

First-Week Program

(90 minutes)

Aim   To relate the subject of forgiveness to our own lives. Participants should have read Chapter 1.

Educational Plan   1. Introduction. Assign participants to review the main ideas of Chapter 1, asking for personal comments on the ground rules. (10 minutes)
2. As a consciousness-raising exercise, have participants complete Exercises 1 and 2. (30 minutes)
3. Divide participants into smaller groups to complete and then to discuss Exercise 4. (20 minutes)
4. Bring your group together to do and discuss the first section of Exercise 5. Ask members of your group to complete Exercise 5 at home. (20 minutes)

Conclusion   Close with a recitation of the Our Father, but with the group adding "Forgive us our trespasses" after each of the seven petitions, e.g., Our Father who art in heaven, "forgive us our trespasses"; Hallowed be thy name, "forgive us our trespasses." (10 minutes)

Second-Week Program

(90 minutes)

Aim To become aware of the steps of the forgiveness process.

Materials needed: The morning newspaper provided by you or by your students/group participants.
Participants should have read Chapter 2.

Educational Plan
1. Introduction. Review the introduction to Chapter 2 and outline the steps in the process of forgiveness. Are there steps missing? Is the order of steps agreeable to your group? What changes do they suggest? (30 minutes)
2. Divide participants into smaller groups with their newspapers. Ask participants to consider where forgiveness is needed or might be the appropriate response in the stories presented. Return to larger group to pool suggestions. (30 minutes)
3. As a consciousness-raising exercise, ask your group to do Exercise 10, "Forgiving Ourselves." (15 minutes)
4. Do Exercise 9, "How Others Have Forgiven," with your group assembled together. Ask for other examples of forgivers. (10 minutes)

Conclusion Read through the Prayer for Peace of St. Francis (page 32) in Exercise 11. (5 minutes)

Third-Week Program

(90 minutes)

Aim   To gain insight and clarify misunderstandings about forgiveness.

Participants should have read Chapter 3.

Educational Plan

1. Introduction. Ask participants to explain briefly each of the five misunderstandings listed in Chapter 3. Are there other misunderstandings that your group would like to add? (10 minutes)

2. Read the Gospel of Luke 15:11–32 with your group. This is the story of the prodigal son. Consider with your group who has to forgive whom in this story. Who is the greatest forgiver and why? (30 minutes)

3. With your group still together, ask participants to do privately Exercise 12, pages 38–39. (10 minutes)

4. Take newsprint or chalkboard to list participants' suggestions regarding the rewards of forgiveness *for the forgiver*. (20 minutes)

5. Exercise 13 should tie together much of the foregoing discussion on misunderstandings. Ask your group to break into small sections to do that exercise. Pool brief reports from each group. (15 minutes)

Conclusion   Close with a reading of the four quotes from Exercise 14 (Menninger, Eliot, Schiller, and King). (5 minutes)

Fourth-Week
Program

(90 minutes)

Aim To relate to obstacles in the forgiveness process. Participants should have read Chapter 4.

Educational Plan
1. Introduction. Ask participants to give a concrete example of each of the obstacles (not ones used in the book). (20 minutes)
2. As a consciousness-raising exercise, ask participants privately to do Exercise 19, "People Who Don't Deserve Forgiveness," pages 55–57. (10 minutes)
3. Cluster participants into small groups. Ask participants to spend fifteen minutes with Exercise 21; then pool suggestions. Ask participants to spend fifteen minutes with Exercise 22; then pool suggestions. (total 30 minutes)
4. Ask participants to volunteer a "case" from the responses to no. 1 above to discuss in terms of forgiveness opportunities through obstacles. Make this a group effort. (20 minutes)

Conclusion Close by reading through Exercise 20 with your group, "Forgiving God," pages 58–59. (10 minutes)

Fifth-Week Program

(90 minutes)

Aim   To appreciate God's forgiveness.

Participants should have read Chapter 5. A copy of the Bible would be helpful for each participant.

Educational Plan   1. Introduction. Ask participants to outline briefly the contents of the introduction to Chapter 5.

Pg. 73

   a. Is God's forgiveness different from our forgiveness?
   b. If God's forgiveness is ours to imitate, what does that mean?
   c. In Matt. 18:21–22, Peter asks Christ, "Lord, how often must I forgive . . . ? As often as seven times?" Jesus answered, "Not seven, I tell you, but seventy-seven times." Can you give examples of this? Followers of Jesus Christ are asked to forgive seventy-seven times. What does that mean? (30 minutes)

2. For private reflection, ask your participants to do Exercise 23, "Testing for Truth," pages 69–70. (10 minutes)

3. Exercise 25, "Where We Need Forgiveness," is an excellent small-group project. After your participants have assembled in small clusters, ask them to complete this exercise. Then pool their comments with the entire group. (30 minutes)

4. While the participants are gathered together, do Exercise 26 with them. (10 minutes)

Add question: Are These 7 sins gender-related? some would argue that These sins (7) are men's. If so, what would be the women's?

Conclusion   Read the Gospel of John 8:1–11. Have participants exchange a sign of peace with each other. (10 minutes)

Supplement:
Sacramental
Program

FIRST PENANCE/ RECONCILIATION

You are forgiven! *Right now, without bargaining, groveling, getting dressed up, doing anything to merit it, or even asking for it*, you are forgiven! *The only thing left is to make God's forgiveness* real *in your life by* accepting it.
Chapter 5, God's Forgiveness

The sacrament is called "penance" or "reconciliation," but the truth it deals with is God's forgiveness—a forgiveness that is so magnanimous, so total, and so unconditional that we have every reason to celebrate it.

As a catechist, you will want to

1. Awaken a sense of awe at God's forgiveness (see Chapter 5 and Exercises 2, 3, 4, 5, 9, 11, 12, 18, 19, 23, 24, 25, 26, 27) by looking at how God forgave in the Old and New Testaments and how he continues to forgive even now.

2. It may be helpful for you to recognize that the preparation for this sacrament circles around three theological themes:

sin   *forgiveness*   *reconciliation*

Each of these themes flows from the other, just as it does in daily life. When you hurt me, I will have to forgive you before our reconciliation takes place. Unfortunately, people (young and old) have a tendency to ignore or bypass step 2 (forgiveness) and to rush into reconciliation. When that happens in connection with the sacrament of penance and reconciliation, we miss the opportunity of savoring the goodness of God, who loves us with a special kind of love that enables him to separate us from our sins and to begin our relationship again without any strings attached.

Simply said, it is your task as catechist to keep a focus on how God forgives and how we go about accepting that forgiveness. It is a focusing that will bear good fruit in lifelong experiences of the sacrament of reconciliation because it will continue to speak to real, not manufactured, spiritual needs that have the ring of truth about them.

3. Involve the families of those in preparation for the sacrament. Adults, especially, who are involved with their children's preparation for penance/reconciliation will appreciate many of the insights in this book. They will understand
- how hard it is to forgive;
- how hard it is to receive forgiveness;
- how forgiveness makes us look weak;
- how desperate some relationships are for the gift of forgiveness;
- how many times we have all been asked to be peacemakers in family, neighborhood, and job situations;
- how God's forgiveness needs to be made more real in our lives.

Parents will be enriched and will become more understanding coeducators of their children when they can relate the power of this sacrament "to start again," to places and persons in their own lives where "starting over" was exactly what was called for.

What the sacrament of penance and reconciliation says, simply, is that no events of human life, even those that turn out badly, are beyond repair. There isn't a member of your parents' group—in fact, there probably isn't a single person you know—who doesn't need to hear that message again. Yours is the privileged task of spreading that very good news.

Procedure In addition to the exercises in the book, a special exercise, *Sacramental Signs of Forgiveness*, follows.

SACRAMENTAL SIGNS OF FORGIVENESS

Religious rites and rituals celebrating forgiveness use signs, too. Frequently, these signs identify so completely with the reality expressed that they effect what they signify. Often, they are so archetypal that they do not even need to be explained.

Baptism is the first among these signs. Through the use of darkness, light, water, and oil, baptism evokes a death as real as Christ's through a dying to our old self and the promise of new life in the community that Christ established.

Perhaps the most transparent sacrament or sign of forgiveness is the Eucharist. Whenever a Christian community receives Communion, this sacrament says without any doubt that our God is a forgiving God. For centuries, the Eucharist was *the* sacrament that signified forgiveness of postbaptismal sin. That teaching still needs to be recovered for our growth as believers and for the sake of the Christian community.

Some Christian denominations have ritualized reconciliation as a separate sign. For Roman Catholics, that sign has sacramental significance and their *New Rite of Penance* (1974) has realigned itself with the very rich theology of penance by making its effective signs more obvious than before. The *New Rite* takes seriously its responsibility to convey corporate sin, the intimacy of forgiving love, community, reunion in community, and conversion as an ongoing event. It is revealing that Rites B and C of the *New Rite* have gained far wider participatory acceptance than Rite A, which is individually directed.

96

It would be a mistake, however, to think that Roman Catholics are alone in seeking forms of forgiveness other than baptism and the Eucharist. The 1973 *Lutheran Book of Worship* includes a Rite of Reconciliation similar in structure and spirit to the *New Rite of Penance* (1974) approved by the Roman Catholic Church. The Anglican *Book of Common Prayer* likewise attends to reconciliation as a separate sign. The Baptist preacher, John R. Claypool, once reflected: "Protestants talked a great deal about the forgiveness of God, but we forgot how *to do* confession and repentance and the receiving of forgiveness." That insight sums up a growing interest among denominations other than Roman Catholics in rites and rituals celebrating forgiveness in a religious context.

If you are involved with the "doing" or the ritualizing of signs of forgiveness and reconciliation, you know how important it is to find signs that are effective and transparent conveyors of the truth of God's love.

The following are signs that others have found helpful. You are free, of course, to adapt them as you see fit to meet the needs of the people you serve.

Anointing   This is a common and an effective sign of healing. In your liturgical service, suggest that participants choose which sense they want anointed as a special sign of where wholeness needs to be recovered in their lives.

Preaching A homily that explains the biblical connection between sin and disease and forgiveness and health.

Suggested Texts Mark 6:12–13—"So they set off to preach repentance; and they cast out many devils, and anointed many sick people with oil and cured them."

James 5:14—"If one of you is ill, he [she] should send for the elders of the church, and they must anoint him [her] with oil in the name of the Lord and pray over him [her]."

Hosea 11:3—"I took them in my arms; yet they have not understood that I was the one looking after them."

Darkness and Light Variations on the theme of darkness and light might include physical darkness in the church representing our unredeemed or sinful

97

state alternating with light representing Redemption and Grace. In providing an opportunity for participants to experience darkness, encourage them to meet and live with themselves through that symbolism. Then suggest meeting God in the brightness and light. Candles can be lit at the beginning of the service, then snuffed while participants reflect on their sinfulness, then lit again in celebration of God's forgiveness.

Preaching A homily dealing with the need to bring light into the dark corners of our hearts.

Suggested Texts Matt. 5:13–16—"You are the light of the world."

Isaiah 58:1–11—". . . if you give your bread to the hungry, and relief to the oppressed, your light will rise in the darkness, and your shadows become like noon."

Eph. 2:1–10—"But God loved us with so much love that he was generous with his mercy: when we were dead through our sins, he brought us to life with Christ."

Eph. 5:1–14—"You were darkness once, but now you are light in the Lord; be like children of light."

Stones   Ask participants in the service to carry two stones—one in each hand—throughout the ritual. The effort will be cumbersome (and appropriately so) while turning pages, standing, sitting, genuflecting, exchanging a handshake, peace greeting. The final release of the stones into a basket near the altar or upon the altar itself would enhance the sign of liberation and freedom.

Preaching A homily dealing with the burden of sin and the freedom of God's forgiving love.

Suggested Texts Luke 15:11–32—"While he was still a long way off, his father saw him and was moved with pity. He ran to the boy, clasped him in his arms and kissed him tenderly."

Romans 6:2–13—"We are dead to sin, so how can we continue to live in it?"

Trash Bag   Present participants at a liturgical service celebrating forgiveness with a brown, sandwich-size bag filled with trash (twigs, an empty, pint-size milk container, rumpled newspaper, etc.) to symbolize the "baggage" we carry around with us all day. Dumping the bag of trash into a receptacle in the back (or front) of the church would signify the surrender of our "baggage" and our willingness to accept and to live a new life of peace.

Preaching A homily dealing with the honesty we all need to identify our sinfulness or a homily dealing with God's activity, through Jesus Christ, in taking our sins away.

Suggested Texts Gal. 5:16–24—"If you are guided by the Spirit you will be in no danger of yielding to self-indulgence."
Luke 15:11–32—"Then he came to his senses."

Plants and Seeds   Presenting participants with a small plant (or a packet of seeds) at the end of a liturgical service could symbolize a fresh start and a new life.

Straw and Flowers   At the beginning of the liturgical service of forgiveness, give each participant a piece of straw. On exiting, trade the piece of straw for a flower.

Preaching A homily on hope, new life, peace, encouragement.

Suggested Texts John 8:1–11—"Go away and don't sin any more."
Romans 12:1-2, 9–19—"Do not model yourselves on the behavior of the world around you, but let your behavior change, modeled by your new mind."

Pebbles   At the beginning of Lent, give each member of the community a plastic "baggie" (sandwich size) containing forty pebbles (fish-tank variety). There are, of course, forty days in Lent. Explain that each pebble symbolizes a sin in our lives for which we have been forgiven or for which we are asking forgiveness. One way to celebrate Lent is to toss away a pebble a day (commemorating a sin remembered each day) celebrating God's love and acceptance of us by forgiving our sins.

Preaching A homily on conversion as an ongoing event, on the purgative experience of Lent, on the mercy of God.

Suggested Texts Luke 18:9-14—"God, be merciful to me, a sinner."

John 15:1-8—"Every branch in me that bears no fruit he cuts away, and every branch that does bear fruit he prunes to make it bear even more."

Tearing Paper Tear up slips of paper on which people have written an event of the past they would like forgiven.

Preaching A homily on healing, repentance, or on our responsibility to help others grow in holiness.

Suggested Texts Luke 17:1-4—"If your brother [sister] does something wrong, reprove him [her] and if he [she] is sorry, forgive him [her]."

Matt. 3:1-12—"Repent, for the kingdom of heaven is close at hand."

Further Readings Joseph M. Champlin, *Together in Peace*. Notre Dame, Indiana: Ave Maria Press, 1975. (Priest's Edition & Penitent's Edition.)

Joseph M. Champlin and Brian A. Haggerty, *Together in Peace for Children*. Notre Dame, Indiana: Ave Maria Press, 1976.

William J. Freburger and James E. Haas, *The Forgiving Christ: A Book of Penitential Celebrations*. Notre Dame, Indiana: Ave Maria Press, 1977.

William J. Koplik and Joan Brady, *Celebrating Forgiveness*. Mystic, Connecticut: XXIII Publications, 1981.

Maria Rabalais, C.S.J., Howard Hall, and David Vavasseur, *Come, Be Reconciled!* Ramsey, New Jersey: Paulist Press, 1975.

Bibliography

On Forgiveness and Reconciliation

Arendt, Hannah. *The Human Condition*. Chicago: University of Chicago Press, 1958. Pages 236–243.

[A provocative few pages on the subject of forgiveness indicating its power and potential.]

Bonhoeffer, Dietrich. *Life Together*. New York: Harper and Row, 1954.

[Not to be missed is Chapter V, "Confession and Communion," Bonhoeffer's pastoral and theological understanding of the need to confess our sins to another Christian and to minister Christ's promise of forgiveness in this context.]

ten Boom, Carrie. *The Hiding Place*. Old Tappan, N.J.: Fleming H. Revell, 1971.

[A moving account written by a Dutch Christian woman of her experiences in a Nazi concentration camp during World War II. The author deals directly with the subject of forgiveness: we are able to sense the ramifications of the subject for the Jewish people.]

Donnelly, Doris. *Learning to Forgive*. New York: Macmillan Publishing Co., Inc., 1979.

[This author's previous work dealing with "Why People Don't Forgive," "What Happens When People Don't Forgive," "What Enables Forgiveness," and other topics.]

Dostoyevsky, Feodor. *The Idiot*. New York: New American Library, 1969 edition.

[A passionately written novel whose main character, Prince Myshkin, is distinguished by his capacity to forgive.]

Frankl, Viktor E. *The Will to Meaning*. New York: New American Library, 1969.

[A gripping memoir of Frankl's survival strategy, through logotherapy, in the Nazi concentration camps of World War II.]

Guest, Judith. *Ordinary People*. New York: Viking Press, 1976.

[An insightful story of a mother incapable of forgiveness and a father and son who struggle with its necessity.]

Haley, Alex. *Roots*. New York: Doubleday & Company, 1974.

[The author raises the thorny subject of racial prejudice and the need for forgiveness of the oppressors of the Blacks.]

Hawthorne, Nathaniel. *The Scarlet Letter*. New York: Random House Modern Library edition, 1926.

[A sensitive and beautiful story that tells of a community that did not know how to forgive and the double standard that condemns and punishes some and exonerates others.]

King, Martin Luther, Jr. "Loving Your Enemies," in *Strength to Love*. New York: Pocket Books, 1964. Pages 47–55.

[A superb sermon that raises and answers two questions: How do we love our enemies? and Why should we love our enemies?]

Klassen, William. *The Forgiving Community*. Philadelphia: Westminster Press, 1966.

[An excellent study that situates the subject of forgiveness in a scriptural and psychological context.]

Menninger, Karl. *Whatever Became of Sin?* New York: Hawthorn Books, 1973.

[A readable and provocative analysis of what occasions the practice of forgiveness.]

Telfer, William *The Forgiveness of Sins*. London: SCM Press, Ltd., 1959.

[An excellent survey of the history of forgiveness and reconciliation in an ecclesial setting. Readable and engaging.]

Webster, Alan. *Broken Bones May Joy: Studies in Reconciliation and Resurrection*. London: SCM Press, Ltd., 1968.

[An original (though mostly theological) approach to forgiveness.]

On Peace Cosby, Gordon and Bill Price. *Handbook for World Peacemaker Groups*. Washington, D.C.: World Peacemakers, n.d.

Haessly, Jacqueline. *Peacemaking: Family Activities for Justice and Peace*. New York and New Jersey: Paulist Press, 1980.

National Conference of Catholic Bishops. *Justice in the World*. Washington, D.C.: United States Catholic Conference, 1971.

Task Force on Christian Education for World Peace. *Teaching Toward a Faithful Vision*. Nashville: Disciples Resources, 1977.

United Presbyterian Church in the United States of America. *Peacemaking: The Believers' Calling*. New York: United Presbyterian Church in the United States of America, 1980.

Scriptural References

The Scriptures below correspond to quotations and references in the text of this book and are compiled here for the convenience of homilists, educators, clergy, and liturgists as well as for those who follow a lectionary or seek to know the sense of the words of the Bible as they pertain to forgiveness, reconciliation, and peace.

Psalm 38:3   "[There is] no soundness in my flesh. . . ." P. 66.

41:4   " 'Cure me, for I have sinned against you.' " P. 66.

51:8   ". . . let the bones you have crushed rejoice again." P. 66.

103:12   "He takes our sins farther away than the east is from the west." P. 66.

120:6–7   "Too long have I lived among people who hate peace. . . ." P. 6.

Isaiah 1:18   " 'Your sins . . . shall be as white as snow. . . .' " P. 66.

2:4   ". . . swords into plowshares." P. 5.

11:6   ". . . calf and lion cub feed together. . . ." P. 8.

58:1–11   ". . . your light will rise in the darkness. . . ." P. 98.

Jeremiah 6:14 " 'Peace! peace!' they say, but there is no peace." P. 29.

Hosea 11:3   "I took them in my arms. . . ." P. 97.

Jonah 3:8   " '. . . let everyone renounce his [her] evil behavior. . . .' " P. 55.

Micah 7:18   "What God can compare . . . pardoning crime . . ." Pp. 31, 68.

Matthew 3:1–12 " 'Repent, for the kingdom of heaven is close at hand.' " P. 100.

5:7   " 'Happy the merciful: they shall have mercy shown them.' " P. 26.

5:9   " 'Happy the peacemakers.' " P. 54.

Index